I0830784

For He Comes Out of Prison to be King

The Gospel of Troy

BOOK 3

Chronicles of the KING

Antionelle Owens

Kingdom Builders Publications LLC

Authored by
Antionelle Owens

Editor
Lakisha S. Forrester
Kingdom Builders Publications

Cover Design
Eric F. Quzack
LoMar Designs

DEDICATION

THIS BOOK IS DEDICATED TO THE KING WHICH DWELLS
WITHIN THE HEART OF ALL THINGS.

INTRODUCTION

Captured, imprisoned within each of us is a "GREATER" that is always seeking to break free, reign over our lives, and continually raise us to our maximum potential. Instead of chains of steel and bars of iron, chains of anger, pride, negative thinking, and bars of social conditioning imprison this "GREATER" and buries it so deep in some that it never manages to get even a glimpse of light, and thus none ever witness it. This phenomena takes place not only in individuals, but in families, races, companies, nations, and every other group. For all groups are ultimately formed of individuals. Thus, it is the purpose of For He Comes Out of Prison to be King to serve as both a documentation of that "GREATER" in the author breaking free and rising to the surface, as well as a call and guide to that "GREATER" which exists in all of those who read its pages.

Out of the darkness, he shall come,

And out of the darkness, he shall lead them,

For he comes out of prison to be KING,

Although he was once forsaken in his kingdom.

CONTENTS

ACKNOWLEDGMENTS

To all who believed (You know who you are), I thank you for your belief. For it gave me the STRENGTH to carry on during my darkest hours. To all who didn't believe (You know who you are), for the exact same reason, I thank you for your disbelief.

I

OUT OF THE DARKNESS, HE SHALL COME

THE PEOPLE THAT WALKED IN DARKNESS HAVE SEEN A GREAT

LIGHT: THEY THAT DWELL IN THE LAND OF THE SHADOW OF

DEATH, UPON THEM HATH THE LIGHT SHINED.

(ISAIAH 9:2)

THE NIGHT IS ALWAYS THE DARKEST IN THE HOUR BEFORE THE DAWN. BUT FEAR NOT, FOR **I AM** THE **KING** OF THE DARKNESS. BEHOLD, I COME UNTO YOU AS A VOICE CRYING OUT FROM THE SILENT DARKNESS OF THE NIGHT. AS A LIGHT FLASHING FORTH FROM THE VOID, IN ORDER TO ILLUMINATE AND MAKE KNOWN THAT WHICH IS AS YET NOT SEEN. JUST AS THE MORNING STAR ARISES FROM THE DARK HORIZON SO THAT IT MAY LIGHT THE WORLD WITH ITS EFFULGENT GLOW OF GOODNESS, SO TOO DO I COME FORTH FROM THE SHADOWS WITH A ROYAL MESSAGE OF REGALITY, SO THAT I, LIKE THE MORNING STAR, MAY LIGHT THE WORLD WITH BEAUTIFUL RAYS OF NOBLE MAGNANIMOUS **KNOWLEDGE** AND **UNDERSTANDING**. AS THE LIGHT, IT IS ONLY FITTING THAT I COME FORTH UNTO YOU FROM THE DARKNESS. FOR WHERE ELSE COULD THE LIGHT, THE **KING** OF THE DARKNESS COME, BUT FROM THE DARK? THUS, THESE WORDS COME TO YOU FROM THE DARKEST PLACE IN THE LAND. FOR MY VOICE CRIES OUT TO YOU FROM THE BELLY OF THE BEAST. FROM THE BOWELS OF PRISON WHERE THE DARKNESS IS **KING**.

FOOLISH PRIDE

Tell me why you choose to dwell in the vain hearts
of foolish men,
And cause the arrogant to be happier with a loss
instead of a win.
Your importance cannot be denied, for you drive us
to success,
However, your destructiveness cannot be discounted,
for so many fail your tests.
So powerful, you caused an angel to be cast down
from above,
So seductive, even the strongest of hearts have
drowned in your LOVE.
You're a facilitator of suffering, the originator of
sin,
The fundamental sustenance of the demons within.
You're an energizer of action, an illusory opener of
the way,
Obstacles can only be transcended when you are
taken out of play.
The weight of your fetters makes it impossible to
soar,
While your deceptive enticements make you difficult
to ignore.

HUBRIS IS THE GREATEST TRAITOR KNOWN TO **FOOLISH PRIDE** MANKIND. FOR HUBRIS MAKES A FOOL OUT OF EVEN THE GREATEST OF MEN. DUE TO HUBRIS, A MAN SHALL INSULT HIS FRIENDS, IMPRUDENTLY BEFRIEND THOSE THAT WOULD BETRAY HIM, AND THROW SCORN UPON THOSE THINGS THAT WOULD AID HIM THE MOST. THERE IS NOTHING THAT CAN COMPARE TO THE **POWER** OF INFINITY. NOR IS THERE ANYTHING THAT CAN PARALLEL THE **WISDOM** OF ETERNITY. HUBRIS IS THE MOST FOOLISH THING IMAGINABLE. **KNOWLEDGE** IS BOUNDLESS. THUS, THERE SHALL ALWAYS BE THINGS THAT YOU DO NOT KNOW. THERE SHALL ALWAYS BE SOMETHING TO LEARN AND SOMEONE TO LEARN FROM. ONLY A FOOL WOULD DARE TO BELIEVE DIFFERENTLY. ONLY A FOOL WOULD BELIEVE THE PERJURY OF HUBRIS.

TELL ME WHY YOU CHOOSE TO DWELL IN THE VAIN HEARTS OF FOOLISH MEN

VAIN IS THE HEART THAT IS FILLED WITH PRIDE. AND FULL OF PRIDE IS THE HEART OF A FOOLISH MAN. BLINDED BY THE DELUSION OF THEIR OWN VANITY, FOOLISH MEN ARE

THOSE WHO BELIEVE THEMSELVES TO BE ABOVE CORRECTION. BECAUSE THEY FEEL INFALLIBLE IN THEIR JUDGMENTS, THEY ARE INCAPABLE OF ENACTING THEIR OWN AMELIORATION. EVEN WHEN PROVEN WRONG IN THEIR ASSESSMENTS, A PRIDEFUL MAN SHALL REFUSE TO ACCEPT RESPONSIBILITY FOR HIS MISTAKES. CHOOSING INSTEAD TO MAKE EXCUSES AND BLAME OTHERS FOR HIS OWN FAULTS, IN THE HOPE THAT HIS HAUGHTY DISPLAY MAY DISTRACT ATTENTION AWAY FROM HIS SHORTCOMINGS. THE REASON THAT PRIDE CHOOSES TO DWELL IN THE VAIN HEARTS OF FOOLISH MEN IS THAT, IN THE HEARTS OF THE WISE, THERE IS NO ROOM FOR PRIDE. FOR THE HEARTS OF THE WISE ARE FILLED WITH HUMILITY.

AND CAUSE THE ARROGANT TO BE HAPPIER WITH A LOSS INSTEAD OF A WIN

PRIDE, THAT GRAND ILLUSIONIST, SHALL CAUSE THOSE MYSTIFIED BY ITS SPELL TO SACRIFICE EVEN THEIR OWN LIFE IN ORDER TO ABATE ITS UNQUENCHABLE DESIRES. THIS IS SOMETHING THAT I HAVE SEEN FIRST-HAND NUMEROUS TIMES DURING MY TIME IN PRISON. ONE TIME IN PARTICULAR THAT STANDS OUT IN MY MEMORY IS WHEN I WITNESSED A MAN GET STABBED OVER TWENTY TIMES,

BECAUSE INSTEAD OF ADMITTING HUMBLY THAT HE WAS WRONG, HE INSTEAD ALLOWED HIS PRIDE TO PERSUADE HIM THAT IT WOULD BE BETTER TO DON A MASK OF ARROGANT CONTEMPT. THIS MAN, WHOM I SHALL CALL TREY, WAS IN CHARGE OF PACKING UP INMATES' PROPERTY FROM HIS DORM WHO HAD TO GO TO LOCKUP. LOCKUP IS WHERE THOSE INMATES WHO COMMIT SERIOUS RULE VIOLATIONS IN PRISON HAVE TO GO FOR A PERIOD OF TIME FOR PUNISHMENT. WHILE PACKING UP ONE INMATE'S PROPERTY IN PARTICULAR, WHOM I SHALL CALL RICO, TREY CAME ACROSS RICO'S RADIO. ALLOWING HIS GREED, WHICH IS AN OFFSPRING OF PRIDE, TO GET THE BEST OF HIM, TREY DECIDED THAT HE WOULD KEEP RICO'S RADIO FOR HIMSELF SO THAT HE COULD SELL IT.

PRIDE IS THE FATHER OF ALL LIES. TREY ALLOWED HIMSELF TO BELIEVE PRIDE WHEN IT WHISPERED TO HIM THAT RICO WOULD PROBABLY GET TRANSFERRED TO ANOTHER YARD AND HE WOULD NEVER HAVE TO SEE HIM AGAIN TO ANSWER FOR HIS TRANSGRESSIONS. WHILE THIS OFTEN DOES HAPPEN WHEN AN INMATE GOES TO LOCKUP, IN THIS CASE, IT WAS FOOLISH FOR TREY TO ASSUME THAT THIS WOULD SAVE HIM

FROM HIS SINS. FOR BOTH HE AND RICO WERE SERVING MULTIPLE LIFE SENTENCES. ANYONE WHO HAS DONE TIME IN PRISON BEFORE KNOWS THAT EVENTUALLY, EVEN IF IT MAY TAKE YEARS, IF YOU HAVE A LIFE SENTENCE YOU SHALL SEE THE SAME FACES AGAIN, IF THEY ARE STILL IN PRISON. IN THIS CASE, RICO DID NOT GET TRANSFERRED. IT ONLY TOOK HIM A COUPLE OF MONTHS TO COME OFF LOCKUP AND RUN INTO TREY ON THE YARD. HUMBLY HE CAME UP TO TREY AND ASKED HIM WHAT WAS UP WITH HIS RADIO. TREY, WHO HAD LONG AGO SINCE SOLD THE RADIO, APPARENTLY TOOK RICO'S HUMILITY FOR WEAKNESS, AS THE ARROGANT OFTEN DO. INSTEAD OF HUMBLY ADMITTING HIS FAULT, APOLOGIZING, AND MAKING AMENDS WITH RICO FOR HIS WEAKNESS SHOWN IN SUCCUMBING TO HIS GREED, TREY INSOLENTLY TOLD RICO, "I TOOK THAT SHIT, NIGGA. I DONE DID THAT." RICO IMMEDIATELY PULLED OUT A LAWN MOWER BLADE SO LONG THAT IT WAS QUITE SHOCKING TO ME THAT HE COULD FIT IT INTO HIS PANTS AND WALK AROUND WITH IT UNNOTICED. TREY, WHO APPARENTLY WAS SHOCKED AS WELL, THREW HIS HANDS UP AND BEGAN TO BACKPEDAL WITH A LOOK OF INTENSE FEAR IN HIS EYES. AS HE TRIPPED AND FELL, AND RICO COMMENCED TO STABBING

HIM, I COULD SEE IN HIS EYES THE DEEP REGRET THAT THE PRIDEFUL ALWAYS FEEL ONCE THEY REALIZE THAT THE BEGUILEMENTS THAT THEIR HUBRIS CONVINCED THEM WERE TRUE WERE NAUGHT BUT LIES.

YOUR IMPORTANCE CANNOT BE DENIED, FOR YOU DRIVE US TO SUCCESS

PRIDE, IN AND OF ITSELF, IS NOT A BAD THING. IT IS ONLY WHEN ONE BECOMES PRIDEFUL, OR ARROGANT, THAT THEY SHALL BRING DESTRUCTION UPON THEMSELVES AND THOSE AROUND THEM. ARROGANCE OCCURS WHEN ONE BELIEVES THEMSELVES ABOVE THE WHOLE. HUMILITY IS WHEN ONE REALIZES THAT THEY AND THE WHOLE ARE ONE IN THE SAME. ARROGANCE CAUSES ONE TO TAKE PRIDE IN THEIR ABILITY TO MANIPULATE THE WHOLE TO THEIR ADVANTAGE. HUMILITY CAUSES ONE TO TAKE PRIDE IN THEIR ABILITY TO HARMONIZE ADVANTAGEOUSLY WITH THE WHOLE. ARROGANCE CAUSES ONE TO BELIEVE THAT THEIR POSITION PLACES THEM ABOVE EVERYONE ELSE. HUMILITY CAUSES ONE TO UNDERSTAND THAT THEY MUST USE THEIR POSITION TO UPLIFT EVERYONE ELSE. ARROGANCE CAUSES ONE TO TAKE PRIDE IN THEMSELVES AND DISMISS THE ACCOMPLISHMENTS OF

OTHERS. HUMILITY CAUSES ONE TO REALIZE THAT ALL PLAY BUT A MINISCULE PART IN THE LORD'S GLORIOUS CREATION. IT IS IMPOSSIBLE TO ATTAIN SUCCESS IN ANY ENDEAVOR WITHOUT TAKING PRIDE IN YOUR OWN INHERENT GREATNESS AND QUALITY OF WORK. HOWEVER, WHEN YOU ALLOW YOUR POSITIVE QUALITIES AND ATTRIBUTES TO CAUSE YOU TO LOOK DOWN UPON OTHERS, YOUR VERY OWN ARROGANCE SHALL BE THE AUTHOR OF YOUR DEMISE. THERE IS NO GREAT AND THERE IS NO SMALL IN THE MIND THAT GAVE BIRTH TO ALL.

HOWEVER, YOUR DESTRUCTIVENESS CANNOT BE DISCOUNTED, FOR SO MANY FAIL YOUR TESTS

MANY MORE PEOPLE FAIL THE TESTS OF SUCCESS, THAN FAIL THE TESTS OF ADVERSITY. ANYTIME ONE ATTAINS TO ANY LEVEL OF **POWER** AND SUCCESS, PRIDE SHALL COME IN ORDER TO TEST THEIR INTEGRITY. FILLING A MAN WITH SUCCESS AND **POWER** IS LIKE FILLING AN EMPTY VASE WITH WATER. BEFORE YOU PUT WATER IN THE VASE, NONE OF HIS IMPERFECTIONS SHALL BE APPARENT. HOWEVER, ONCE THAT VASE IS FILLED, ANY HOLES OR CRACKS THAT WERE HIDDEN IN THE STRUCTURE OF THAT VASE SHALL BECOME EVIDENT TO

ALL. IN THE SAME WAY, BEFORE A MAN HAS ATTAINED **POWER** AND SUCCESS, THOSE IMPERFECTIONS THAT HE HAS IN HIS CHARACTER SHALL BE HIDDEN BY THE INVISIBILITY OF HIS OBSCURITY. HOWEVER, ONCE HE IS FILLED WITH **POWER**, ANY FLAWS THAT HE HAS IN THE CONSTITUTION OF HIS NATURE SHALL POUR FORTH TO THE DETRIMENT OF ALL. THE GREATER THE **POWER** THAT A MAN POSSESSES, THE MORE DAMAGE HE SHALL BE ABLE TO DO IF HE IS INFECTED BY ARROGANCE. THE MAIN REQUISITE FOR OBTAINING ULTIMATE **POWER** LIES IN ONE'S ABILITY NOT TO USE IT. THE UNIVERSE, IN ITS ULTIMATE MERCY AND **WISDOM**, SHALL ONLY GRANT ULTIMATE **POWER** TO ONE WHO HAS PURIFIED HIS HEART SUFFICIENTLY OF THE ARROGANCE WHICH OBSCURES ITS LIGHT. NOT ONLY WOULD AN IMPURE HEART DESTROY ITSELF WITH THIS **POWER**, BUT IT WOULD ALSO DESTROY ALL WHICH STANDS AROUND IT. FOR TO GIVE AN ARROGANT PRIDEFUL MAN ULTIMATE **POWER** WOULD BE LIKE GIVING THE CONTROL OF A NUCLEAR BOMB TO AN ADOLESCENT.

SO POWERFUL, YOU CAUSED AN ANGEL TO BE CAST DOWN FROM ABOVE

Lucifer, the light bearer in all of his glory, was duped by hubris into believing that he should be revered over that which was the source of his creation. He allowed his pride to convince him to bring disorder into order, and disharmony into harmony by attempting to upset the natural order of things by placing himself above the position of the progenitor of all that ever was and shall be. For Lucifer to attempt to usurp rule from God would be like a toe attempting to usurp sovereignty of the body from the head. Only confusion could ensue. Because discord has no place in harmony and order, which is what heaven is, Lucifer was cast down so that he may become Satan, the steward of turmoil and disarray, which is what hell is. This is the fate of all who refuse to play their proper part in the body of life due to their envy of the position of another member of the very same body. All of the parts of a body, from the toes to the fingers, are equally significant to the possessor of that body.

For each part has a particular part to play that no other part of that body is able to play. The elbows could never perform the duty of the knees. The neck could never play the part of the ankle. The heart could never do the job of the stomach. However, because each part performs the duty proper to its purpose, the body is able to perform efficiently. Each part is special in its own unique way.

SO SEDUCTIVE, EVEN THE STRONGEST OF HEARTS HAVE DROWNED IN YOUR LOVE

In the ocean of the mind, pride is one of the strongest currents. If one is not careful, it shall easily pull them into a direction that they do not wish to go. All men **LOVE** nothing more than the sweet song of validation and praise. Pride, that seductive sweet voice inside, shall always find willing listeners in those who are unaware of the danger inherent in its deceptive harmony. Just as the mythological sirens would sing to sailors in order to get them to shipwreck, so too shall pride serenade those souls sailing upon the waters of life in order

TO GET THEM TO SHIPWRECK UPON THE ROCKS OF DESPAIR
AND DROWN IN THE WATERS OF GRIEF.

YOU'RE A FACILITATOR OF SUFFERING, THE ORIGINATOR OF SIN

SUFFERING IS A RESULT OF EXPECTATIONS. EXPECTATIONS
COME FROM THE FEELING THAT SOMETHING SHOULD, OR IS
SUPPOSED TO HAPPEN, EXACTLY THE WAY THAT ONE WANTS
IT TO HAPPEN. INSTEAD OF ACCEPTING THINGS AS THEY
ARE, SEEING THE PERFECTION THAT IS LIFE, AND
HARMONIZING WITH CIRCUMSTANCES, A PRIDEFUL MAN ONLY
SEES HIS OWN EXPECTATIONS, AND PROBLEMS WITH HOW
THINGS ARE. THINGS CAN ONLY GO THE WAY THAT THEY'RE
SUPPOSED TO GO. IN REALITY, YOU HAVE DUALITY. IN
DUALITY, THERE ARE TWO NATURES. THERE IS THE SUPERIOR
NATURE, WHICH IS ETERNAL AND UNCHANGING, AND THERE
IS THE MATERIAL NATURE, WHICH IS TEMPORARY AND WHOSE
VERY NATURE IS CHANGE ITSELF. SUPERIOR NATURE IS THE
NATURE OF THE SPIRIT. MATERIAL NATURE IS THE NATURE
OF THE WORLD. BOTH NATURES ARE FOUND IN REALITY,
THEREFORE BOTH NATURES ARE REAL. THE NATURE OF THE
SPIRIT SHALL ALWAYS BE SUPERIOR TO THE NATURE OF THE
WORLD BECAUSE IT IS ETERNAL. THE WISE MAN WHO

POSSESSES TRUE **UNDERSTANDING** SHALL HUMBLY SURRENDER TO, BOW BEFORE, AND SERVE THE SUPERIOR NATURE. AS A RESULT OF HIS SUBMISSION, ALL OF MATERIAL NATURE SHALL BOW TO AND SERVE HIM. FOR HE HAS ALIGNED HIMSELF WITH, AND BECOME THE AMBASSADOR OF THAT WHICH RULES ALL. ARROGANT MEN SHALL ATTEMPT TO RULE MATERIAL NATURE, AND AS A RESULT OF HIS EFFORTS, MATERIAL NATURE SHALL TYRANNIZE HIM. TO ATTEMPT TO CONTROL MATERIAL NATURE IS AS VAIN AS ATTEMPTING TO CHASE THE WIND. THE PRIDEFUL, BECAUSE THEY CAN ONLY SEE THE SURFACE LEVEL OF THINGS, SHALL ALWAYS BE RULED BY THAT WHICH THEIR PHYSICAL EYES CAN SEE. THEY SHALL ALWAYS ATTEMPT TO HOLD ON TO THAT WHICH IS TEMPORARY AND IGNORE THAT WHICH IS ETERNAL. NEVER **UNDERSTANDING** THAT WHICH IS ETERNAL IS THE SOURCE OF THE TEMPORARY.

THE FUNDAMENTAL SUSTENANCE OF THE DEMONS WITHIN

ONE'S INNER DEMONS ARE NOURISHED AND NURTURED BY THE VILE AMBROSIA OF PRIDE. PRIDE IS THAT WHICH CAUSES ONE TO TAKE OFFENSE TO, RESENT THE ACTIONS OF OTHERS,

AND SEEK REVENGE. IT IS PRIDE THAT CAUSES ONE TO REJECT **KNOWLEDGE** WHICH MAY BE BENEFICIAL TO THEM, AND WILLINGLY REMAIN IN THE DARKNESS OF IGNORANCE. IT IS PRIDE THAT CAUSES ONE TO LOOK AT ANOTHER AND BECOME ENVIOUS OF THEM. THE DEMONS OF RESENTMENT, ENVY, IGNORANCE, AND ALL OF THEIR RESULTING OFFSPRING, ARE FED AND SUSTAINED BY PRIDE AND PRIDE ALONE.

YOU'RE AN ENERGIZER OF ACTION, AN ILLUSORY OPENER OF THE WAY

IT IS AN UNDENIABLE FACT THAT PRIDE IS WHAT ENERGIZES AND PROPELS ONE TO ACCOMPLISH GREAT THINGS. HOWEVER, WHEN ONE ALLOWS THEMSELVES TO BELIEVE THAT IT IS THEM AND THEIR PRIDE THAT ARE EXCLUSIVELY RESPONSIBLE FOR THE GOODNESS IN THEIR LIFE, THEY HAVE ALLOWED THEMSELVES TO BE MISLED BY THE ILLUSION OF MATERIAL NATURE. SPIRIT IS RESPONSIBLE FOR ALL THAT HAPPENS TO A MAN. ALL THAT A MAN DOES IS PLANT THE SEEDS OF THAT WHICH HE DESIRES TO GROW. BECAUSE OF THE LAW, A MAN SHOULD NEVER PLANT APPLE SEEDS AND GET CORN, NOR SHALL ORANGE SEEDS EVER PRODUCE PINEAPPLES. HOWEVER, A MAN SHALL NEVER HAVE CONTROL OVER THE

DETAIL OF THE PLANTS THAT SHALL BE PRODUCED BY THOSE SEEDS WHICH HE PLANTS. FOR WHILE A MAN MAY INDEED PLANT APPLE SEEDS, HE KNOWS NOT HOW MANY APPLES THAT APPLE TREE SHALL PRODUCE, HOW LONG IT SHALL TAKE TO MATURE, OR EVEN IF IT SHALL GROW APPLES AT ALL. THESE THINGS ARE GRANTED BY THE GRACE OF NATURE. IT WOULD BE QUITE FOOLISH FOR A MAN TO CLAIM DIRECT RESPONSIBILITY AND TAKE EXCLUSIVE CREDIT FOR THE GROWING OF AN APPLE TREE AND THE CROP OF APPLES THAT IT PRODUCES, WITHOUT ACKNOWLEDGING THE SOIL, THE RAIN, THE SUNSHINE, AND THE LAW OF NATURE ITSELF, WHEN ALL HE DID WAS PUT SEEDS IN THE GROUND. IN THE SAME WAY, IT IS FOOLISH FOR A MAN TO TAKE EXCLUSIVE CREDIT FOR THE EFFECTS THAT TAKE PLACE IN HIS LIFE, WHEN ALL HE HAD TO DO WAS PLANT THE SEEDS. THE ONLY THING THAT HE MAY TAKE CREDIT FOR IS THE PLANTING OF THE PROPER SEEDS. THE SPROUTING OF THE SEEDS THEMSELVES, AS WELL AS ALL THAT IS PRODUCED FROM THOSE SEEDS, IS DUE ENTIRELY TO GRACE. TO UNDERSTAND THIS IS TO RID ONESELF OF FALSE PRIDE AND REMAIN IN A STATE OF PERPETUAL GRATITUDE.

OBSTACLES CAN ONLY BE TRANSCENDED WHEN YOU ARE TAKEN OUT OF PLAY

TO THE HUMBLE MAN, THERE ARE NO OBSTACLES. THERE ARE ONLY CAMOUFLAGED BLESSINGS AND STEPPING STONES TO GREATNESS. WHILE THE PRIDEFUL MAN LAMENTS AND RAILS MISERABLY AGAINST HIS FATE, THE HUMBLE MAN EMBRACES IT AND LOOKS CONSTANTLY FOR THE DISGUISED OPPORTUNITIES THAT ADVERSITY SHALL ALWAYS DELIVER. WHEN SOMEONE IS RUDE TO A PRIDEFUL MAN, THE PRIDEFUL MAN IS OFFENDED, RESENTS THE RUDENESS OF THE PERSON, AND MAKES AN ENEMY OF THAT PERSON BY RESPONDING IN KIND. WHEN SOMEONE IS RUDE TO A HUMBLE MAN, THE HUMBLE MAN VIEWS THIS AS AN OPPORTUNITY TO DISPLAY THE NOBLE QUALITIES OF MAGNANIMITY AND POISE, AND PROVE HIMSELF SUPERIOR TO THOSE IGNOBLE FEELINGS OF RESENTMENT THAT ARISE WITHIN HIMSELF. THE HUMBLE MAN DOES THIS WITH THE **UNDERSTANDING** THAT THE WICKED SHALL ALWAYS EVENTUALLY BOW BEFORE THE RIGHTEOUS. FOR IT IS THE NATURE OF THE LIGHT TO SUBJUGATE THE DARKNESS. IN LIFE, IT SHALL ALWAYS BE MORE EFFICIENT TO BE COURTEOUS THAN TO DISPLAY VULGAR RUDENESS, NO MATTER WHAT THE CIRCUMSTANCE.

For courtesy allows one to harmonize advantageously with the workings of the whole, while rudeness produces friction and discord. Pride shall prevent one from seeing the opportunities present in each moment by directing the attention of the prideful man to those things that he does not like in those moments. All like opportunity. Thus, it shall never be possible to see opportunity if one is always focused upon those things that they dislike.

THE WEIGHT OF YOUR FETTERS MAKES IT IMPOSSIBLE TO SOAR

The manacles of pride shackle one to the world, making it impossible for one to soar to the elevations of spirit. Pride distracts one from the faultless perfection that is the concordant nature of the universe by instead placing one's attention upon temporary phenomena that are but evanescent illusions. All phenomena of the universe come into being, stay for a while, and then fade away never to return again. When one becomes attached to one of these mirages, pain inevitably follows. It is this pain

THAT CAUSES ONE TO CURSE THAT WHICH IS IMPECCABLE. THIS IS THE EPITOME OF ARROGANCE. FOR ONLY AN ARROGANT MAN WOULD DARE TO CRITICIZE THAT WHICH IS PERFECT. IT IS THIS ARROGANCE THAT KEEPS ONE FROM SOARING. IT IS IMPOSSIBLE TO FLY FREELY WHEN ONE IS ENSLAVED BY PAIN.

WHILE YOUR DECEPTIVE ENTICEMENTS MAKE YOU DIFFICULT TO IGNORE

PRIDE IS THE GREATEST DECEIVER OF MAN. FOR PRIDE IS CAPABLE OF CONVINCING A MAN TO LIE TO HIMSELF. PRIDE SHALL PERSUADE A MAN TO BELIEVE THAT WHAT IS NOT, INDEED SHOULD BE, AND WHAT IS, INDEED SHOULD NOT BE. YOUR PRIDE IS JUST AS INTELLIGENT AS YOU ARE. THEREFORE, IT KNOWS EXACTLY WHICH DECEPTIONS SHALL WORK TO THE BEST EFFECT. PRIDE, AN AUTONOMOUS FORCE OF THE UNIVERSE, IS ALWAYS LOOKING TO CONTROL THE WEAK, SO THAT IT MAY GROW MORE POWERFUL. IT SHALL USE WHATEVER MEANS NECESSARY TO ACCOMPLISH THIS. THE GREATER THE PRIDE THAT A MAN IS ABLE TO CONTROL WITHIN HIMSELF, THE MORE HUMBLE, AND HENCE MORE POWERFUL THAT MAN SHALL BECOME. THE WISE LOOK UPON PRIDE, NOT

AS AN ENEMY TO BE ANNIHILATED, BUT AS AN OPPONENT WHICH PROVIDES ONE WITH THE MEANS TO GAIN **STRENGTH** OF CHARACTER. THE **STRENGTH** OF CHARACTER THAT ONE GAINS FROM OVERCOMING PRIDE MANIFESTS ITSELF AS POISE, TEMPERANCE, SERENITY, MAGNANIMITY, UNSELFISHNESS, AND ALL OTHER NOBLE AND ROYAL ATTRIBUTES. THESE ATTRIBUTES DO NOT COME CHEAP. IF THEY DID, THEN THEY WOULD NOT BE VALUABLE.

THE INTERNAL FLAME

Scorching hot, an eternal fire,

Unforgivingly cold, sparked by

malevolent desire.

You cloud the vision of your victims,

and make their decisions rash,

Never far away, often you come in a

flash.

Without you, there is peace, although

some LOVE your feeling,

You send patience and kindness away,

compassion you send reeling.

A perilous source of POWER, so

difficult you are to control,

A scorching conflagration, your

voracity consumes souls.

THE INTERNAL FLAME

Anger, the twin brother of pride, is a fire that dwells in the hearts of all men. Just as pride cannot be justly labeled an evil thing in and of itself, so anger cannot justly be called evil in and of itself. Like the element of fire, it can only be considered to be an evil thing if it rages unrestrained. There is a major difference between feeling anger and possessing it, and becoming angry and being possessed by it. Feeling anger is like a fire in a fireplace, whereas becoming angry is like a raging wildfire. While one is controlled and beneficial, the other is uncontrollable and destroys all that stands in his path.

SCORCHING HOT, AN ETERNAL FIRE

Fire, perhaps the most beautiful and powerful of all the elements, creates as readily as it destroys. Think of the fires in space known as stars. They provide light and life to the universe. Without the sun, life on Earth as we know it, could not exist. Fire sterilizes and burns away all of those things that are

INCAPABLE OF WITHSTANDING ITS FURY. THINK OF EXERCISING. ONE KNOWS THAT THEIR WORKOUT IS EFFECTIVE BY THE BURN THAT THEY FEEL. THIS PAIN IS WHAT INFORMS ONE THAT THE WORKOUT IS BURNING AWAY THE USELESS MATERIAL THAT THEY WISH TO RID THEMSELVES OF. THINK OF THE PRECIOUS METAL GOLD. WHEN IT IS BEING PROCESSED, FIRE IS USED TO BURN AWAY ITS IMPURITIES. THE FIRE OF ANGER CAN BE USED IN THE SAME WAY IF ONE IS STRONG ENOUGH TO CONTROL IT. WHEN ANGER THREATENS TO OVERTAKE ONE'S MIND, IF THEY ARE ABLE TO REMAIN CONSCIOUS AND NOT BECOME POSSESSED BY IT, THEY CAN USE ITS ENERGY TO PROPEL THEM TO THE GREATEST OF HEIGHTS. JUST AS THE FIRE OF A ROCKET PROPELS IT TO THE HEAVENS. IN MY OWN EXPERIENCE IN PRISON, I HAVE BEEN ABLE TO USE THE FIRE OF THE ANGER THAT ARISES IN MY SPIRIT TO PURIFY ME OF MY VAPIDITY, AND FUEL MY QUEST FOR MAGNIFICENCE. BECAUSE I CONSCIOUSLY DO THIS, **I AM** ABLE TO USE THE FLAMES OF MY WRATH TO BURN AWAY THE WEAKNESSES IN MY CHARACTER, WHICH ALLOW THE RAGE TO ARISE IN THE FIRST PLACE. PAIN IS WEAKNESS LEAVING ONE'S SPIRIT. THUS, THIS PROCESS CAN BE A PAINFUL ONE. HOWEVER, LIKE

WORKING OUT, THE MORE I DO THIS, THE MORE ENDURANCE I GAIN. THE MORE ENDURANCE I GAIN, THE MORE **I AM** ABLE TO HANDLE. THE MORE **I AM** ABLE TO HANDLE, THE MORE POWERFUL I BECOME. WHEN ONE TURNS AN ENEMY INTO A HELPER, THAT ENEMY IS DESTROYED. ANGER IS DEFEATED WHEN ONE IS ABLE TO SEE THAT THE PURPOSE OF ANGER IS TO REVEAL TO THEM WEAKNESSES IN THEIR CHARACTER WHICH NEED TO BE ERADICATED IN ORDER FOR THEM TO TAKE THEIR PLACE AMONGST THE GREAT.

UNFORGIVINGLY COLD, SPARKED BY MALEVOLENT DESIRE

THERE IS NOTHING COLDER AND UNFORGIVING THAN A PERSON FULLY IN THE GRIPS OF THEIR ANGER. REVENGE, A DISH BEST SERVED COLD,[1] IS SIMMERED BY MALEVOLENTLY FRIGID FIRES OF RESENTMENT. RESENTMENT, IN TURN, IS SPARKED BY THE ANGER THAT NATURALLY ARISES WHEN ONE FEELS THAT THEY HAVE BEEN TRANSGRESSED UPON. THERE WAS ONE INCIDENT IN PARTICULAR THAT OCCURRED DURING MY TIME IN PRISON THAT EPITOMIZES THIS SITUATION

---

[1] English proverb from the 1800s.

PERFECTLY. THERE WAS A MAN, WHOM I SHALL CALL BK, WHO SERVED IN THE CAPACITY OF WHEELCHAIR PUSHER FOR HIS DORM. THOSE WHO SERVED AS WHEELCHAIR PUSHERS WERE EMPLOYED BY MEDICAL TO CHAUFFEUR THOSE INMATES WHO WERE INCAPACITATED AND UNABLE TO WALK BACK AND FORTH TO THEIR DESTINATIONS WITHOUT ASSISTANCE. THERE WAS ONE MAN IN PARTICULAR, WHOM I SHALL CALL RED, WHO BK PUSHED AROUND ALL DAY ON A DAILY BASIS. OVER TIME, THE TWO FORMED AN AMICABLE RELATIONSHIP. ONE DAY, BETWEEN THEM, AN ARGUMENT ENSUED OVER SOME SORT OF FINANCIAL MATTER THAT THE TWO MEN WERE INVOLVED IN. IN THE HEAT OF THE ARGUMENT, RED ANGRILY TOLD BK TO SUCK HIS DICK. AS ANYONE WHO HAS EVER BEEN TO PRISON KNOWS, THIS IS A TRANSGRESSION OF MOMENTOUS PROPORTIONS. WHEN RED UTTERED THESE FILTHY WORDS, EVERYONE SURROUNDING THEM INSTANTLY HUSHED IN ANTICIPATION OF THE VIOLENCE THAT ALL WERE CERTAIN WAS ABOUT TO ENSUE. HOWEVER, BK, SEEMINGLY TAKING THE PROVERBIAL HIGH ROAD IN THE SITUATION, SIMPLY NODDED HIS HEAD AND SAID, "OKAY, I'LL SUCK YOUR DICK," AND WALKED AWAY. WHILE INDEED THERE WERE SOME WHO WITNESSED THIS INCIDENT THAT WERE thinking that BK had punked out, there were others that were relieved that he had walked away, as everyone knew that the two laughed and talked every day. Days went by and it seemed that everything had blown over and BK had let the whole thing go. However, one day as Red was sitting unsuspecting in his wheelchair on the rock talking to another inmate and watching a card game being played, BK ran up and shouted out, "You wanted me to suck your dick, huh?" He then kicked Red's wheelchair over, jumped on top of him, and commenced to stabbing him to death right there in Uncontrolled rage front of everyone.

YOU CLOUD THE VISION OF YOUR VICTIMS, AND MAKE THEIR DECISIONS RASH

The harbinger of regret, makes victims by turning everything that one perceives into an enemy, and blinding one to the consequences of their actions. Blind anger causes want to speak indiscreetly and act imprudently. This shall never be a positive thing in any endeavor. Discretion and prudence are the most

IMPORTANT POSSESSIONS THAT ANY MAN COULD EVER ACQUIRE. FOR WITHOUT THESE, NO UNDERTAKING CAN ATTAIN ANY KIND OF ENDURING SUCCESS. DISCRETION AND PRUDENCE BESTOW UPON A MAN THE **POWER** TO CONTROL HIMSELF AND ALL THAT SURROUNDS HIM, BY BESTOWING UPON HIM THE ABILITY TO REACT APPROPRIATELY TO ALL CIRCUMSTANCES WHICH MAY COME AGAINST HIM. BLIND RAGE DOES NAUGHT BUT SWINDLE THESE PRECIOUS ATTRIBUTES FROM THE MINDS OF ITS VICTIMS. THUS, IT SHALL ALWAYS BE CONSIDERED TO BE **THE GREATEST ADVERSARY OF GREATNESS.**

NEVER FAR AWAY, OFTEN YOU COME IN A FLASH

ANGER IS ALWAYS LURKING IN THE SHADOWS, WAITING FOR THE OPPORTUNITY TO SEIZE CONTROL OF THE HEART OF ITS UNSUSPECTING PREY. LIKE A WAVE OF A TSUNAMI, OR THE WIND OF A HURRICANE, ANGER SHALL SWEEP AWAY THE WILL OF HE WHO HAS NOT TETHERED HIS MIND TO THE PILLAR OF FOCUS WITHIN HIMSELF. TO BE SWEPT AWAY BY ANGER IS TO DROWN IN THE WATERS OF CONTRITION. FOR ANGER, LIKE PRIDE, IS AN AUTONOMOUS FORCE THAT SHALL SPREAD

PERDITION AND RUIN WHEREVER IT IS ALLOWED TO REIGN
UNCHECKED.

WITHOUT YOU, THERE IS PEACE, ALTHOUGH SOME LOVE YOUR FEELING

ALTHOUGH ANGER IS INDEED SUBVERSIVE, THE FRAUDULENT
FEELING OF **POWER** THAT IT INFUSES ONE WITH CAN BE
INTOXICATING AND HIGHLY ADDICTIVE. ONE GETS ANGRY
BECAUSE THE ANGER CONVINCES THEM THAT IT IS ABLE TO
SOLVE THE PERCEIVED PROBLEM THAT TROUBLES THEM. FOR
EVERY ACTION, THERE IS AN EQUAL AND OPPOSITE
REACTION.[2] THE VIRULENT ENERGY THAT IS ANGER SHALL
ALWAYS RETURN BACK TO ITS SOURCE WITH THE SAME FORCE
WITH WHICH IT WAS EXPELLED. WHILE AN EMOTIONAL
OUTBURST OF TEMPER MAY INTIMIDATE AND COW SOME FOR
A WHILE, THE LACK OF RESPECT THAT RESULTS FROM THE
LACK OF CONTROL EXHIBITED SHALL ULTIMATELY NULLIFY
AND OFFSET ANY ADVANTAGES GAINED. ACTIONS
PERFORMED IN THE SPIRIT OF ANGER, NO MATTER THE
APPEARANCE OF THE IMMEDIATE EFFECTS, SHALL INEVITABLY
BE DETRIMENTAL TO THE PERFORMER OF THOSE ACTS IN

---

[2] Newton, Isaac. 1687. *Philosophiae Naturalis Principia Mathematica.*

TIME. FOR ONE CAN ONLY REAP THAT WHICH ONE SOWS.

YOU SEND PATIENCE AND KINDNESS AWAY, COMPASSION YOU SEND REELING

WHEN ANGER TAKES POSSESSION OF ONE'S MIND, THE VIRTUES THAT DEFINE NOBILITY OF MIND DEPART, AND IMPATIENCE, MALICE, AND CRUELTY, VICES THAT DEFINE IGNOMINY, INFILTRATE. NOT ONLY SHALL THESE VICES DESECRATE AND CONTAMINATE THE MIND WHICH THEY OCCUPY, BUT THEY SHALL ALSO POLLUTE THE ENVIRONMENT WHICH SURROUNDS THAT MIND.

A PERILOUS SOURCE OF POWER, SO DIFFICULT YOU ARE TO CONTROL

THE GREATEST WAY TO CONTROL ONE'S ANGER IS TO GAIN THE ABILITY TO IGNORE THE PRIDE WHICH FUELS IT. THIS IS THE ESSENCE OF HUMILITY. WITHOUT HUMILITY, THERE SHALL ALWAYS BE CONTENTION AND STRIFE. IN THE PRESENCE OF CONTENTION AND STRIFE, THERE SHALL ALWAYS BE ENEMIES. IN WAR, THE ONLY ONE THAT IS CERTAIN TO PREVAIL IS THE ONE THAT HAS NOT AN ENEMY. HUMILITY IS THE RECOGNITION THAT EVERYTHING IS LIFE. EVERYTHING THAT COMES TO ONE, COMES TO ONE IN LIFE, AND IS LIFE

ITSELF. TO OPPOSE ANYTHING IN LIFE IS TO OPPOSE LIFE ITSELF. THE ESSENCE OF **WISDOM** IS THE ABILITY TO FLOW WITH LIFE, AND USE ALL THAT COMES TO ONE IN LIFE, TO ONE'S ADVANTAGE. ANGER PREVENTS ONE FROM DOING THIS. FOR ANGER CREATES OPPOSITION SO THAT IT MAY DESTROY INSTEAD OF UTILIZE, AND RAVAGE INSTEAD OF RENDER USEFUL.

A SCORCHING CONFLAGRATION, YOUR VORACITY CONSUMES SOULS

RIGHT NOW, AS I WRITE THIS VERY PASSAGE, THE RAVENOUS FIRES OF RAGE THREATEN TO DEVOUR MY GOODNESS AND LEAVE ONLY THE ASHES OF BITTERNESS BEHIND. WE HAVE BEEN LOCKED IN OUR ROOMS FOR TWO WEEKS AND COUNTING. WE HAVE BEEN DENIED SHOWERS FOR THESE TWO WEEKS AND HAVE YET TO BE FED TODAY. NOT BECAUSE OF ANY INFRACTION THAT HAS TAKEN PLACE AT THE INSTITUTION, BUT BECAUSE WE HAVE A NEW WARDEN WHO IS TRYING TO MAKE A NAME FOR HIMSELF AND ESTABLISH A REPUTATION FOR BEING TOUGH AT OUR EXPENSE. AS HUNGER PANGS REVERBERATE THROUGH MY STOMACH, THOUGHTS OF WISHING HARM UPON THE NEW WARDEN,

AND IMAGES OF HIM BEING HARMED FLIT PERSISTENTLY THROUGH MY MIND. INDEED, THE THOUGHT THAT THE WARDEN SEES US NOT AS HUMAN, BUT AS A MEANS TO AGGRANDIZE HIS OWN STATUS, SPARKS AN ANTIPATHY INSIDE OF ME INCOMPREHENSIBLE TO ANYONE WHO HAS NOT BEEN SUBJECTED TO THE SAME TREATMENT. HOWEVER, MY **UNDERSTANDING** THAT MY TRIBULATIONS ARE TOUGHENING ME AND MAKING ME MORE POWERFUL, FORTIFIES MY HEART AND PROVIDES IT WITH THE DETERMINATION AND **STRENGTH** TO OVERCOME THE ACRIMONY THAT SEEKS TO DECIMATE THE GOODNESS AND HUMANITY THAT ILLUMINATE IT.

II

AND OUT OF THE DARKNESS, HE SHALL LEAD THEM

ARISE, SHINE; FOR THY LIGHT IS COME, AND THE GLORY OF

THE LORD IS RISEN UPON THEE.

(ISAIAH 60:1)

All life on Earth are expressions or manifestations of the infinite energy known as **BEING**, which composes the entire universe. As human **BEINGS**, we possess the unique gift of being able to express or manifest this energy in whatever manner that we choose. You see, whereas a cat is a cat, and can only be a cat, and nothing else, a human **BEING** can be a doctor, priest, beggar, zookeeper, or any other number of things. Humans have the ability to shape their own characters, master their own wills, and direct their own lives. This is what the beautiful gift of free will bestows upon us. Unfortunately, in the society of today, this truth goes largely untaught. Consequently, most grow up ignorant of their true potential as a human **BEING**. All men were born to be kings. Kings of their families. Kings of their neighborhoods. Kings of their households. Kings of their nations. Kingship is indeed the foundation of every success that a man wishes to attain in this life.

The dictionary defines a **KING** as "a person or thing

REGARDED AS THE FINEST OR MOST IMPORTANT IN ITS

SPHERE OR GROUP."[3] IN SHORT, A LEADER. BEFORE

ANYTHING ELSE, THIS IS WHAT THE MEN OF THE WORLD

MUST BECOME. EVERYTHING ELSE IS SECONDARY. IT IS THIS

MESSAGE THAT I COME TO YOU BEARING. IT IS THIS

MAJESTIC LAMP OF NOBLENESS WHICH I SHINE SO THAT ALL

WHO WISH TO FOLLOW MAY USE MY LIGHT AS A GUIDE TO

DIRECT THEM TO THEIR TRUE DESTINIES AS MEN.

---

[3] https://www.lexico.com/definition/king

1

WE MUST STAND. FOR WE ARE AT WAR.

(A talk given at McCormick Correctional Institution)

Peace, brothers. Last year, about a day or so after I gave my talk on the subject of purpose, I was sitting in contemplation in the cafeteria when a wise man came to the table at which I was seated and said, "You know, that was real good what you said about the kings and all, but there comes a time when all kings must lead their people to war." So it is on this day, my fellow kings, I come to you with a message so dire that I can only pray that **I AM** able to adequately convey its significance. For today, brothers, it has fallen upon me to alert you that we are under attack, and we must all declare war or we shall all be annihilated. But the enemy lies not out there, brothers, as we have all been tricked into believing. Oh, no. You see, the enemy that we as kings must defeat is hiding right here in our very own minds. For the most diabolical and wicked adversary that we shall ever face is none other than our very own ignorance. To be conquered by

IGNORANCE IS THE MOST VILE AND SHAMEFUL DEFEAT THAT A **KING** COULD EVER SUFFER. FOR TO BE CONQUERED BY IGNORANCE IS TO BE DEFEATED BY NONE OTHER THAN ONESELF. AND THIS, BROTHERS, TO BE DEFEATED BY ONESELF, IS A MOST PATHETIC AND PITIFUL THING. NOW THIS BATTLE AGAINST IGNORANCE IS ONE THAT WE ALL HAVE LOST. AS A RESULT OF OUR FAILURE, WE HAVE ALL BEEN FORCED TO PAY A PRICE THAT IS MUCH TOO HIGH. FOR AS A RESULT OF OUR DEFEAT, WE HAVE ALL BEEN FORCED TO FORFEIT OUR FREEDOM. AND WHAT, BROTHERS, COULD POSSIBLY BE MORE VALUABLE THAN OUR FREEDOM? BUT ALAS, I SAY UNTO YOU, DO NOT LOSE HEART. ALTHOUGH WE MAY HAVE BEEN DEFEATED BY OUR OWN IGNORANCE IN THE PAST, KEEP IN MIND THAT SOMETIMES IT IS BETTER TO LOSE A BATTLE IN ONE'S YOUTH, SO THAT ONE MAY WIN THE WAR WHEN THEY GROW OLD.

ESPECIALLY USEFUL IN TIMES OF WAR IS COURAGE. COURAGE IS THE GREATEST **POWER** OF ALL. FOR IT IS COURAGE THAT FREES THE MIND FROM THE ENSLAVEMENT OF THE EMOTIONS, AND TAKES AWAY NOT ONLY FEAR, BUT EVEN THE AWARENESS OF DANGER. TWO OTHER ESSENTIAL QUALITIES

THAT YOU MUST POSSESS IN ORDER TO WIN WAR ARE DETERMINATION AND PATIENCE. THESE VIRTUES LEAD TO A SPIRIT THAT IS RESOLUTE AND IMPERVIOUS TO ANY AFFLICTION WHICH LIFE MAY DELIVER. AND THERE SHALL BE AFFLICTIONS, BROTHERS. MANY OF THEM. FOR IN THE PROCESS OF GAINING **WISDOM**, THERE SHALL BE MUCH GRIEF. HOWEVER, THIS WAR ON IGNORANCE, NO MATTER HOW MUCH PAIN IT MAY CAUSE US, IS ONE WHICH WE MUST NOT AVOID. FOR WAR, WHEN IT IS NECESSARY, IS NEVER TO BE AVOIDED. TO ATTEMPT TO AVOID IT IS TO ONLY DELAY IT, TO THE ADVANTAGE OF YOUR ENEMIES.

KINGS, IT IS OF THE UTMOST IMPORTANCE THAT WE GAIN **WISDOM**. IT IS ONLY THE WISE THAT ARE ABLE TO DISCERN THE POISONS AND TRAPS THAT LIE HIDDEN IN ALL OF THE AFFAIRS AND CIRCUMSTANCES OF LIFE. **WISDOM** IS THE ONLY RELIABLE AMMUNITION TO USE AGAINST THE ADVERSARY OF IGNORANCE. SO AS I STAND BEFORE YOU ALL TODAY, IT IS MY MOST SINCERE WISH THAT I MAY BE ABLE TO ASSIST YOU IN THIS MOST HEROIC ENDEAVOR BY PROVIDING YOU WITH ARTILLERY, SO THAT YOU MAY BE BETTER ABLE TO EFFECTIVELY WAGE YOUR OWN WAR. HOWEVER, BEFORE I

BEGIN, I MUST STRESS TO YOU WITH THE UTMOST GRAVITY THAT ALTHOUGH ON THIS DAY I SHALL BE SHARING WITH YOU A PORTION OF MY OWN PERSONAL **WISDOM**, IN WAR, BEING UNCONQUERABLE LIES SOLELY WITHIN ONESELF. THUS, ONE MUST RELY PRIMARILY UPON THEIR OWN FORCES. WHILE YOU SHOULD OBTAIN FACTS, INFORMATION, AND COUNSEL FROM OTHERS, YOU MUST ALWAYS RETAIN THE RIGHT TO ACCEPT OR REJECT SUCH COUNSEL, EITHER IN WHOLE OR IN PART, AS YOU SEE FIT. UNDER NO CIRCUMSTANCES ARE YOU EVER TO ALLOW ANYONE TO DO YOUR THINKING FOR YOU. TO DO OTHERWISE IS TO ALLOW ANOTHER TO RULE YOUR KINGDOM.

FIRST AND FOREMOST, ONE THING THAT YOU ALL MUST COME TO UNDERSTAND IS THAT YOU ARE ALL BEINGS OF **POWER**. YOU ARE **POWER** ITSELF, AND THUS THE MASTER OF YOUR OWN THOUGHTS, THE SOLUTION TO ALL OF YOUR OWN PROBLEMS, AND THE POSSESSOR OF THE ABILITY TO TRANSFORM YOURSELF INTO WHATSOEVER YOU MAY DESIRE TO BE. THINK ABOUT THAT FOR A SECOND, BROTHERS. THERE SHOULD BE NO MORE INSPIRING FACT TO YOU THAN THIS. FOR THIS MEANS THAT YOU HAVE THE

ABILITY TO ELEVATE YOUR LIFE BY THE USE OF YOUR VERY OWN THOUGHTS. IN FACT, YOU MUST RID YOURSELF OF ANY THOUGHT WHICH TELLS YOU ANYTHING CONTRARY TO THIS. FOR IN WAR, IT IS ALWAYS BEST TO ELIMINATE ANY WEAPONS THAT DO NOT SERVE YOUR SIDE. FOR REST ASSURED, BEFORE THE WAR IS OVER, ANY WEAPONS THAT DO NOT SERVE YOUR SIDE SHALL BE USED AGAINST YOU.

IN THE BEGINNING, BEFORE THE FIRST OF TIME, WHEN LOVE MADE THE DECISION TO COME FORTH FROM THE UNCREATED IN ORDER TO BRING FORTH MANIFESTATION, IT RECOGNIZED IN ITS INFINITE **WISDOM** THAT BEFORE THIS COULD BE ACCOMPLISHED IT HAD TO FIRST LAY DOWN A UNIVERSAL SET OF IMMUTABLE LAWS, **THE TRUTH**, UPON WHICH ITS CREATIONS COULD BE ESTABLISHED. IT IS **THE TRUTH** THAT SERVES GOD AS BOTH THE CREATOR AND PRESERVER OF THE ORDER AND PEACE THAT ARE THE ESSENTIAL FOUNDATION REQUISITE TO EVERY CREATION.

THAT CAPRICIOUS GODDESS WHICH MEN CALL SUCCESS SHALL ONLY CONSENT TO BE ESCORTED BY THE ORDER, PEACE, AND HARMONIOUS ACTION THAT **THE TRUTH** BRINGS ABOUT. IT SHALL ALWAYS BE SEEN THAT WHEREVER THERE IS

FOUND UNITY, TRANQUILITY, AND CONCORD, THERE SHALL ALSO BE FOUND TRUTH AND LAW. HOWEVER, WHEREVER DISORDER, DISUNITY, AND DESTRUCTION PREVAIL, IT SHALL ALWAYS BE SEEN, WITHOUT FAIL, THAT THERE IS NEITHER TRUTH NOR LAW PRESENT. ONLY LIES AND LAWLESSNESS.

JUST AS IN THE BEGINNING **THE TRUTH** WAS APPOINTED BY GOD TO RULE AND BE **KING** OF THE ENTIRE UNIVERSE, SO TOO HAVE YOU BEEN APPOINTED BY **THE TRUTH** TO RULE YOUR KINGDOMS HERE ON EARTH. AND JUST AS GOD, WITH **THE TRUTH**, BROUGHT FORTH ORDER OUT OF CHAOS AT THE BEGINNING OF CREATION, SO TOO MUST YOU, WITH **THE TRUTH**, BRING FORTH ORDER TO YOUR REALMS. **THE TRUTH** IS A COSMIC FORCE THAT INHERENTLY BRINGS HARMONY AND COHERENCE TO ALL SITUATIONS. IT SHALL ALWAYS BE SEEN THAT WHEN A **KING** RULES HIS KINGDOM WITH **THE TRUTH** AS HIS CHIEF ADVISOR, PEACE SHALL, WITHOUT FAIL, REIGN SUPREME. IN FACT, PEACE IS THE VERY STANDARD OF TRUTH BY WHICH YOU AS A **KING** MUST JUDGE YOUR KINGDOM. FOR GREATNESS SHALL NEVER BE ACHIEVED BY A PEOPLE WITHOUT SOCIAL HARMONY AND ITS

COMPANION, PEACE. BROTHERS, IT IS IN THIS THAT YOU FIND YOUR VERY PURPOSE FOR EXISTENCE.

THE CHIEF DUTY OF A **KING** IN THIS WORLD IS TO UNITE HIS PEOPLE IN HARMONY. IN FACT, TO BE A GREAT **KING** IS TO POSSESS AN **UNDERSTANDING** SO REMARKABLE THAT YOUR VERY PRESENCE IS ENOUGH TO BRING FORTH UNITY AND HARMONY TO ANY SET OF CIRCUMSTANCES. IN TRUTH, A MAN CAN ONLY BE JUSTLY CALLED **KING** IF HE IS CAPABLE OF THIS. THERE SHALL ALWAYS BE A PLACE FOR ONE WHO IS ABLE TO CREATE HARMONY IN HUMAN RELATIONSHIPS. THAT PLACE IS THE THRONE. A TRUE **KING** SHALL ALWAYS BE SEEN BRINGING GRACE AND INTELLIGENCE ALONG WITH HIM. IT IS THESE PRICELESS JEWELS THAT HE GIVES AS GIFTS TO HIS PEOPLE. BECAUSE HE UNDERSTANDS THAT IT IS ALSO HIS DUTY TO BE AN INSPIRATION TO HIS PEOPLE, A TRUE **KING** SHALL ALWAYS SEEK, ABOVE ALL ELSE, TO BE A LIVING STANDARD OF PHYSICAL, MENTAL, AND SPIRITUAL EXCELLENCE.

TRUE KINGS NEED NONE TO CROWN THEM AS SUCH. TRUE KINGS CROWN THEMSELVES BY MEANS OF THEIR WAYS AND ACTIONS. JUST AS ALL WHO WRITE CANNOT JUSTLY BE

CALLED POETS, ALL WHO HOLD A POSITION OF AUTHORITY CANNOT JUSTLY BE CALLED KINGS. A RULER'S LIFE IS ONLY VALUABLE AND GOOD SO LONG AS HE USES HIS POSITION TO ORDER THE COURSE OF NATURE FOR THE BENEFIT OF HIS PEOPLE. A TRUE **KING** SHALL ALWAYS DO EVERYTHING IN HIS **POWER** TO MAKE HIS KINGDOM LIKE THE KINGDOM OF HEAVEN FOR THE SAKE OF ALL THOSE WHO LIVE UNDER HIS RULE. JUST AS IN THE KINGDOM OF THE HEAVENS, THE SUN, MOON, AND STARS REFLECT TO THE WORLD, LIKE A REFLECTION IN THE MIRROR, A CERTAIN RESEMBLANCE OF THE BEAUTY OF GOD, SO TOO ON EARTH, A FAR CLOSER RESEMBLANCE OF THE BEAUTY OF GOD IS REFLECTED BY TRUE KINGS WHO **LOVE** AND VENERATE GOODNESS. EXHIBITING TO THEIR PEOPLE THE RADIANT LIGHT OF MAGNANIMITY, ATTENDED BY A LIKENESS OF THE SUPREME **UNDERSTANDING** OF THE CREATOR. YOU SEE, BROTHERS, IT IS THROUGH KINGS, IT IS THROUGH YOU, THAT GOD DISPLAYS RIGHTEOUSNESS, NOBILITY, PRUDENCE, AND GOODNESS, WHICH SERVE AS A MUCH CLEARER PROOF OF THE **DIVINE** TO THE EYES OF THE MASSES THAN EVEN THE INCANDESCENCE OF THE SUN, THE GRACEFUL GLOW OF THE MOON, OR THE INFINITUDE OF THE TWINKLING STARS.

Just as law and not confusion is the dominating principle of the universe, and justice, not injustice, is the soul and substance of the harmony found in life, so too much is righteousness, and not corruption, be the molding and moving force in the government of your kingdoms.

Kings are, in fact, the keepers and maintainers of righteousness among men upon the Earth. Truly, kingship is the supreme science which every man ought aspire to master. It is only those who have a veritable **UNDERSTANDING** of the science of kingship that possess the **POWER** necessary to bring true peace and concord to their realms, and earn that regal authority which this science bestows upon all its virtuosos. Although many indeed may be labeled as such, it is only those who truly understand how to rule virtuously that are truly kings. While men are able, and do in fact, give **DIGNITY** to titles, titles have not the ability to give **DIGNITY** to men. It shall always be seen that in a land in which an unvirtuous transgressor has

MADE HIMSELF, OR HAS BEEN NAMED **KING**, THAT LAND SHALL BE SO FILLED WITH TRANSGRESSIONS AND TRESPASSES THAT ITS DESTRUCTION SHALL NEVER BE FAR AWAY. RIGHT CAN ONLY BE PROLONGED BY ONE WHO HAS IN THE COFFER OF HIS SPIRIT THE PRICELESS JEWELS OF KINGLY VIRTUE.

KINGS, IT IS PARAMOUNT THAT THE CHARACTER WHICH YOU FASHION FOR YOURSELF BE ONE BUILT UPON A FOUNDATION CONSTRUCTED WITH THE VIRTUOUS PRINCIPLES OF GENEROSITY, COMPASSION, AND HUMILITY. IN ORDER TO BE ONE OF THOSE MAGNIFICENT SOULS THAT TRULY DESERVE THE TITLE OF **KING**, IT IS IMPERATIVE FOR YOU, LIKE THE SUN, TO POSSESS A GIVING NATURE, WHICH IMPARTS LIFE TO ALL THOSE WHOM YOUR LIGHT FALLS UPON. SINCE IT IS ONLY THE MOST SAVAGE OF BEAST THAT RULES SIMPLY BECAUSE THEY ARE THE STRONGEST, IT SHALL ALWAYS BE SEEN THAT TRUE KINGS ARE THE WIELDERS OF A COMPASSION SO INCOMPARABLE THAT IT GIVES THEM THE CAPACITY TO HELP ANY LIVING CREATURE AT ANY GIVEN TIME. A KING'S GENEROSITY AND HIS COMPASSION ARE BUT MERE RAYS OF ILLUMINATION THAT RADIATE FORTH FROM THE LUMINOSITY OF HIS HUMILITY, WHICH IN ITSELF IS BUT A PRODUCT OF HIS

UNDERSTANDING THAT IF ANY WOULD BE THE GREATEST OF ANY GROUP, THEY MUST MAKE THEMSELVES A SERVANT TO THE REST. RESPECT.

2

HE WHO DEFINES, RULES. IN ORDER TO TRULY BE **KING**, YOU MUST RETAIN THE ABILITY TO DEFINE YOURSELF. A **KING** DEFINES HIMSELF. ONE IS ONLY ABLE TO ACCESS THE FULL EXTENT OF THEIR **POWER** BY DEFINING WHO THEY ARE. ALL OF ONE'S **POWER** LIES IN THEIR ABILITY TO DEFINE THEIR OWN REALITY. YOU MUST MAINTAIN THE DETERMINATION TO DEFINE YOURSELF AT ALL COST, NO MATTER HOW CRAZY IT MAY SEEM TO OTHER PEOPLE. YOU CANNOT BE **KING** IF YOU HAVE NOT THE **POWER** TO DEFINE YOURSELF.

RATHER THAN SUCCUMBING TO PARADIGMS FORCED UPON THEIR HEARTS AND MINDS BY OTHERS, KINGS USE THE **POWER** OF THEIR WILL TO FORM THEIR OWN IDEALS AND DIRECTIVES. THEY THEN INSCRIBE THESE REGULATIONS UPON THEIR SPIRIT, AND AS A RESULT ARE ABLE TO IMPEL THE

PSYCHE OF OTHERS DUE TO THE IMMENSE FORCE OF THEIR
RESOLUTION.

THE VAST MAJORITY OF PEOPLE IN THIS WORLD ARE SLAVES
OF HEREDITY AND THEIR ENVIRONMENT, AND MANIFEST VERY
LITTLE FREEDOM OF CHOICE. THEY ARE SWAYED BY THE
OPINIONS, CUSTOMS, AND THOUGHTS OF THE OUTSIDE
WORLD, AND ALSO BY THEIR OWN EMOTIONS, FEELINGS, AND
MOODS. THOSE THAT KNOW AND UNDERSTAND THE LAWS
OF LIFE RISE ABOVE THE PLANE OF PHYSICALITY, PLACE
THEMSELVES IN TOUCH WITH THE HIGHER **POWER** OF
THEIR NATURE, AND DOMINATE THEIR OWN MOODS,
CHARACTER, QUALITIES, AND THINKING, AS WELL AS THE
ENVIRONMENT SURROUNDING THEM. THEY BECOME KINGS
INSTEAD OF PAWNS. CAUSES INSTEAD OF EFFECTS.
WISDOM COMES FROM ONE'S **KNOWLEDGE** OF THE
LAWS OF LIFE. KINGS FALL IN WITH THESE LAWS, LEARN
THEM, AND BY **UNDERSTANDING** THEIR
MOVEMENTS, OPERATE THEM, INSTEAD OF BEING THEIR
BLIND SLAVE. JUST AS THE SKILLED SWIMMER COMPARES TO
THE STICK THAT IS CARRIED HERE AND THERE BY THE WHIM
OF THE WATER, SO DOES THE **KING** COMPARE TO THE

COMMON MAN. AND YET BOTH THE SWIMMER AND THE STICK, THE **KING** AND THE COMMON MAN, ARE SUBJECT TO THE SAME LAWS.

THE LAW OF **DIVINE** ONENESS STATES THAT EVERYTHING IS CONNECTED, AND ALL THAT WE THINK, SAY, DO, AND BELIEVE HAS AN EFFECT. THE LAW OF PERPETUAL TRANSMUTATION OF ENERGY STATES THAT ALL PERSONS HAVE WITHIN THEM THE **POWER** TO CHANGE THEIR CONDITIONS. THE LAW OF ACTION STATES WE MUST ENGAGE IN ACTIONS THAT SUPPORT OUR THOUGHTS, DREAMS, EMOTIONS, AND VISION IN ORDER TO MANIFEST THEM. THE LAW OF VIBRATION STATES THAT EVERYTHING IN THE UNIVERSE IS IN CONSTANT MOTION AND THEREFORE CONSTANTLY CHANGING. THE LAW OF ATTRACTION STATES THAT YOU ATTRACT INTO YOUR REALITY THAT WHAT YOU ARE FOCUSED UPON.

3

MOTION IS THE INHERENT PRINCIPLE UNDERLYING ALL PHENOMENA. VIBRATION IS THE INHERENT PRINCIPLE UNDERLYING ALL MOTION. THE SPEED AT WHICH A

PHENOMENON VIBRATES IS THE DETERMINING FACTOR OF ITS FREQUENCY. THE FREQUENCY OF A PARTICULAR PHENOMENON IS WHAT DETERMINES HOW IT IS PERCEIVED. NOTHING PRESENT WITHIN THE ENTIRE UNIVERSE, NO MATTER HOW STILL IT MAY APPEAR, IS UNMOVING. EVERYTHING CHANGES AND EVERYTHING IS PERPETUALLY CHANGING. THESE CHANGES ARE CYCLIC AND DUE TO THE VIBRATORY NATURE OF ALL PHENOMENA. THE SUPERFICIAL DIFFERENCES BETWEEN THE MYRIAD MANIFESTATIONS OF BEING IS DUE ENTIRELY TO THE INFINITE RATES OF FREQUENCY PRESENT WITHIN INFINITY.

EVERY THOUGHT OR MENTAL STATE HAS ITS CORRESPONDING RATE AND MODE OF OPERATION. BY GAINING KNOWLEDGE OF THE LAW OF VIBRATION, AS APPLIED TO MENTAL PHENOMENA, YOU MAY LEARN TO POLARIZE YOUR MIND AT ANY DEGREE THAT YOU WISH, THEREBY GAINING PERFECT CONTROL OVER YOUR MENTAL STATES AND MOODS. BY UNDERSTANDING THIS LAW THOROUGHLY, YOU MAY POLARIZE YOUR MIND AT A LEVEL OF VIBRATION WHICH CORRESPONDS TO THE RATE OF VIBRATION OF A KING. YOU CAN WIN FREEDOM FROM THE CHAINS OF YOUR

CONDITIONING BY SELF-EFFORT, AND SELF-EFFORT ALONE.
YOUR MIND IS THE BUILDER. YOU BECOME WHAT YOUR
MIND DWELLS UPON. IF YOU ALTER YOUR ATTITUDES AND
MODES OF THOUGHT, AND ATTUNE YOUR CONSCIOUSNESS
TO A HIGHER FREQUENCY BY NOT ONLY HAVING, BUT ALSO
LIVING A HIGHER IDEAL, YOU CAN BE LIBERATED FROM THE
SHACKLES OF BONDAGE THAT SOCIETY HAS PLACED UPON
YOU. YOU CAN BECOME **KING**. YOU HAVE THE
POWER TO TAKE HOLD OF YOUR LIFE AND ACTIVELY SHAPE
YOUR FUTURE.

IN TODAY'S SOCIETY, THE CONSCIOUSNESS OF THE MAJORITY
OF PEOPLE, FROM AN EARLY AGE, ARE DRAWN TOWARDS
DESIRES AND IDEALS THAT PRODUCE IMMENSE AMOUNTS OF
SUFFERING, NOT ONLY FOR THEMSELVES, BUT FOR THEIR
FAMILIES AND COMMUNITIES AS WELL. TELEVISION, RADIO,
NEWSPAPERS, MOVIES, BASICALLY ALL OF POPULAR CULTURE,
WITH SOME ADMIRABLE EXCEPTIONS, DRAW PEOPLE'S
CONSCIOUSNESS IN THE DIRECTION OF ALL TYPES OF IDEALS
THAT LEAD TO MISERY. TO COMPOUND THE PROBLEM, MOST
ARE UNAWARE THAT THIS PROCESS IS EVEN TAKING PLACE.
THEREFORE, MOST ARE BEING UNCONSCIOUSLY PROGRAMMED

TO MOVE IN DIRECTIONS THAT THEY HAVE NO DESIRE TO GO. MOST ARE BEING DRAWN TO DESTRUCTION UNBEKNOWNST TO THEMSELVES. IT IS IN THIS THAT I FOUND MY PURPOSE. FOR IT HAS FALLEN UPON MY SHOULDERS TO HELP AID ANY THAT DESIRE TO STOP THE MOMENTUM TOWARDS IGNOMINY, AND BEGIN TO STEER IT TOWARD THE LUMINOSITY OF EXCELLENCE, BY GIVING ALL WHO WOULD LISTEN, A NEW GOAL. THE MOST NOBLE GOAL OF BECOMING A **KING**.

IN ORDER TO AFFECT A TRUE AND POSITIVE CHANGE IN YOUR EXPERIENCE OF LIFE, YOU MUST DISREGARD HOW YOU THINK THINGS ARE, AS WELL AS HOW OTHERS ARE SEEING YOU, AND DIRECT YOUR ATTENTION EXCLUSIVELY TO THE WAY THAT YOU PREFER THINGS TO BE. BY DELIBERATELY DIRECTING YOUR ATTENTION RATHER THAN MERELY OBSERVING WHAT IS HAPPENING AROUND YOU, YOU SHALL CHANGE YOUR MENTAL VIBRATION BY AN EFFORT OF WILL. BY NO LONGER RESPONDING TO WHAT OTHERS PERCEIVE YOU TO BE, IN TIME YOU SHALL CREATE A FUTURE THAT CORRELATES TO YOUR DESIRES. YOU SHALL BECOME THE **POWER** THAT DELIBERATELY CREATES YOUR OWN EXPERIENCE. WILL

DIRECTS THE ATTENTION, AND ATTENTION DETERMINES THE VIBRATION. TO CULTIVATE THE ART OF ATTENTION BY MEANS OF THE WILL IS TO BECOME **KING**. FOR TO DO THIS IS TO BECOME THE MASTER OF YOUR OWN MIND. UNLESS YOU ACQUIRE THE MASTERY OF THE ART OF CHANGING YOUR OWN VIBRATION, YOU SHALL BE UNABLE TO AFFECT YOUR ENVIRONMENT. AN **UNDERSTANDING** OF THIS PRINCIPLE SHALL ENABLE YOU TO CHANGE YOUR OWN VIBRATION, AS WELL AS THAT OF OTHERS, IF YOU WOULD BUT DEVOTE THE TIME, CARE, STUDY, AND PRACTICE NECESSARY TO MASTER THIS ART. THE PRINCIPLE IS POWERFUL, BUT THE RESULTS OBTAINED DEPEND UPON PERSISTENT PRACTICE AND PATIENCE. FEW REALIZE, OR EVEN FATHOM, THAT THEY CAN CONTROL THE WAY THEY FEEL, AND POSITIVELY AFFECT THAT WHICH ENTERS THEIR LIFE EXPERIENCE BY DELIBERATELY DIRECTING THEIR ATTENTION. JUST LIKE ANYTHING ELSE, IF YOU ARE NOT ACCUSTOMED TO DOING A THING, IT TAKES PRACTICE TO MASTER THE SKILL. YOUR ATTENTION TO ANYTHING DRAWS IT CLOSER TO YOU. THEREFORE, YOUR ATTENTION TO KINGSHIP SHALL DRAW THE CROWN TO YOUR HEAD. TO ATTAIN THE CROWN IS TO BE **KING**. AND AS

KING, THERE IS NOTHING THAT YOU CANNOT BE, DO, OR HAVE.

4

AS YOU BELIEVE, SO SHALL YOU ACT. AS YOU ACT, SO SHALL GO YOUR DESTINY. A BELIEF IS MERELY A THOUGHT THAT ONE CONTINUALLY THINKS. JUST AS YOU CONDITION YOUR BODY IN DIFFERENT WAYS THROUGH EXERCISE, OR THE LACK OF IT, SO TOO DO YOU CONDITION YOUR MIND. EVERY MIND STATE, THOUGHT, OR EMOTION THAT YOU EXPERIENCE REPEATEDLY BECOMES STRONGER AS YOU BECOME MORE HABITUATED TO IT. WHO WE ARE AS PERSONALITIES IS A COLLECTION OF ALL THE TENDENCIES OF MIND THAT HAVE BEEN DEVELOPED. THESE ARE THE PARTICULAR ENERGY CONFIGURATIONS THAT WE HAVE CULTIVATED. EACH THOUGHT THAT ONE THINKS CREATES IMPRESSIONS WITHIN THE MIND OF THE THINKER OF THAT THOUGHT IN SUCH A WAY THAT A DISPOSITIONAL TENDENCY TO REPEAT THE THOUGHT IS LAID DOWN. AMONG THE INDISPENSABLE MEANS TO BECOMING A KING IS ROYAL THINKING AND ROYAL CONDUCT. IT IS BY THE DEGREE AND NATURE OF ROYAL VIRTUE ACHIEVED THAT THE DEGREE OF KINGSHIP MAY

BE ACCESSED, AND THE QUALITY OF KINGSHIP MAY BE EVALUATED. THE TREE IS MADE KNOWN BY ITS FRUITS. JUST AS VARIOUS COMPUTER PROGRAMS MAY BE CREATED TO SIFT INPUT DATA, SO THE MIND IS ABLE TO CREATE AND CHANGE THE COGNITIVE PROGRAMS BY WHICH THE REPORTED SENSORY STIMULI ARE SELECTED, INTERPRETED, AND ACTED UPON. ONE IS ABLE TO REPROGRAM AND RECONSTRUCT THEIR OWN AWARENESS IN LINE WITH THEIR OWN MOTIVATIONS. REPETITION OF A MANTRA, WHICH IS THE FOCUSING OF THE MIND UPON A SINGLE THOUGHT, OR VERBAL IMAGE, IS A MEDITATIVE TECHNIQUE DESIGNED TO DISRUPT THE ORDINARY FILTER AND ACTIVITY OF THE MIND, AND OPEN THE WAY FOR A NEW FRESH PERCEPTION. SUCH A TECHNIQUE LEADS TO A TURNING OFF OF HABITUAL WAYS OF PERCEIVING THE EXTERNAL WORLD, AND A CONSEQUENT OPENING UP OF A NEW STATE OF AWARENESS AND **BEING**.

THE DIVINE KING MANTRA

I AM POWER.

I AM THE TRUTH.

I AM A DIVINE KING.

I AM WISDOM, STRENGTH, FAITH,

KNOWLEDGE, and UNDERSTANDING.

I AM DIGNITY and HONOR.

I AM THE GREATEST KING THAT HAS EVER

LIVED.

For I AM THE MASTER OF POWER.

The universe is responding to the thoughts that you are thinking. It shall not distinguish between a thought brought about by your observation of some reality you have witnessed, and a thought brought about by your imagination. As you ponder whatever thought that you are thinking, the law of attraction goes to work, and begins to offer you other thoughts, conversations, and experiences that are of a similar nature. Your thoughts establish your point of attraction.

Focus is **POWER**. The longer you give your focus to a thought, the more powerful that thought shall become, due entirely to the **POWER** of your focus. The more powerful that thought becomes, the stronger your point of attraction it is to it, and the more evidence of it shall appear in your life experience.

If you focus upon a thought long enough, it shall become your reality. Nothing can be a part of your experience unless you invite it through your attention to it. The magnetic **POWER** of the law

OF ATTRACTION REACHES OUT INTO THE UNIVERSE AND ATTRACTS OTHER THOUGHTS THAT ARE VIBRATIONALLY ATTUNED TO YOUR THOUGHTS, AND BRINGS THE PHYSICAL MANIFESTATION OF THESE THOUGHTS TO YOU. LEARN TO SEE YOURSELF AS A MAGNET WHICH ATTRACTS UNTO HIMSELF THE ESSENCE OF WHAT YOU ARE THINKING AND FEELING. IF YOU CONTINUALLY THINK NOBLE THOUGHTS AND FEEL NOBLE FEELINGS, YOU SHALL ATTRACT NOBILITY UNTO YOURSELF. THE MAGNETIZED SKILLET WHOSE ESSENCE IS OF GOLD SHALL ATTRACT TO ITSELF ANOTHER OBJECT WHOSE ESSENCE IS OF GOLD. A MAN WHOSE ESSENCE, OR MIND, IS OF A ROYAL NATURE SHALL ATTRACT TO HIMSELF A LIFE WHOSE ESSENCE IS ROYAL.

IF YOU WISH FOR THE UNIVERSE TO TREAT YOU AS A **KING**, YOU MUST FEEL, THINK, AND ACT AS A **KING**. YOUR ATTENTION TO SUBJECTS AND YOUR ACTIVATION OF THOUGHTS CONCERNING THOSE SUBJECTS, COMBINED WITH THE LAW OF ATTRACTION'S RESPONSE TO THOSE THOUGHTS, ARE RESPONSIBLE FOR EACH AND EVERY PERSON, EVENT, AND CIRCUMSTANCE THAT COME INTO YOUR EXPERIENCE. ALL OF THESE THINGS COME TO YOU BECAUSE THEY ARE VIBRATIONAL

MATCHES TO THE VIBRATIONAL FREQUENCY THAT YOU YOURSELF ARE EMITTING. YOU SHALL RECEIVE THE ESSENCE OF WHAT YOU ARE THINKING ABOUT. WHETHER IT IS SOMETHING YOU WANT, OR SOMETHING YOU DO NOT WANT. WHEN YOU ARE CLEAR ABOUT EVERYTHING THAT YOU WANT, YOU SHALL RECEIVE ALL THE RESULTS THAT YOU DESIRE. ANY IDEA SHALL MANIFEST ITSELF EXTERNALLY IF ONE'S ATTENTION IS DEEPLY CONCENTRATED UPON IT. RIGHT MOTIVES, FEELINGS, AND THOUGHTS ARE MORE IMPORTANT EVEN THAN RIGHT ACTION. FOR ENERGIES FROM THE HIGHER PLANES ARE MORE POWERFUL THAN PHYSICAL ENERGIES. THUS, THE FIRST AND MOST ESSENTIAL STEP IN BECOMING A **KING** IS TO FIRST HAVE THE MOTIVES, FEELINGS, AND THOUGHTS OF A **KING**. ALL THINGS HAVE BECAUSES. A MAN IS A **KING** BECAUSE HE THINKS AS A **KING** DOES. A MAN IS A **KING** BECAUSE HE FEELS LIKE A **KING**. ALL ARE ARTISTS. BUT INSTEAD OF CANVAS AND PAINT AS OUR MEDIUM, OUR VERY BODIES, MINDS, AND LIFE EXPERIENCES ARE THE MATERIALS OF OUR CREATIVE EXPRESSION.

ONCE A PERSON BEGINS TO VIEW THEMSELVES AS A **KING**,

THAT PERSON SHALL BEGIN TO ACT AS A **KING**. ONCE THIS HAPPENS, THE WORLD SHALL RESPOND TO THAT PERSON AS IT WOULD TO A **KING**. A **KING**, LIKE THE SUN, RADIATES, ENLIGHTENS, NOURISHES, EXPANDS, ENLIVENS, ENRICHES, AND CAUSES THE GROWTH OF EVERYTHING WITHIN ITS CIRCUMFERENCE. A **KING** INCREASES THE VALUE OF ANYTHING HE COMES INTO CONTACT WITH. INDEED, THE WORLD WOULD LITERALLY BECOME A BETTER PLACE IF MORE PEOPLE GENUINELY SOUGHT TO STEP INTO THE SPIRIT OF THIS ARCHETYPAL CHARACTER.

5

YOU ARE ALWAYS IN THE PROCESS OF CREATING YOUR OWN WORLD EXPERIENCE FROM WITHIN. YOU ARE BOTH THE CREATOR OF THE OCCASION, AND THE RESPONDER TO THE OCCASION. WHEN SITUATIONS ARISE AND YOU REACT TO THEM, THOSE REACTIONS DETERMINE YOUR FUTURE. IF YOU REACT TO EVERY SITUATION AS A **KING** WOULD, THEN YOU SHALL HAVE THE FUTURE OF A **KING**. THERE IS NO SEPARATION BETWEEN YOUR INNER AND OUTER REALITY. ONLY YOUR MIND TELLS YOU THERE IS. THAT WHICH YOU ARE IN YOUR HEART, THE WORLD SHALL RESPOND IN KIND.

You are what you think you are. All that you are arises with your thoughts. It is with your thoughts that you create your world. You shall only be able to, if you believe you are able to. Everything arises from your mind. Every thought that you have is instantly felt throughout the entire universe.

Every person shall receive the reverberation of their own thoughts and actions. The consequences of a man's thoughts and deeds must all react upon himself with the same force with which they were set in motion. For equilibrium and harmony can only be restored by the reconversion to the same point all the forces which were set in motion from it. This is law.

You yourself are responsible for your life and all the circumstances, pains, joys, opportunities, and limitations that compose it. Everything you are is the outcome of forces you yourself have set in motion. You are living under the domain of your self-made destiny. Your actions and thoughts enter a continuous rivulet of causation that shall

DETERMINE YOUR FATE. NOTHING IS EVER LOST. ALL OF THE THOUGHTS, MOTIVES, EMOTIONS, AND ACTIONS THAT YOU HAVE GENERATED IN THE PAST HAVE GONE INTO THE COMPLEX ALLOY THAT MAKES YOU WHAT YOU ARE TODAY. IT IS YOU WHO VINDICATE OR CONDEMN YOURSELF. IT IS IMPOSSIBLE TO ERASE THOSE CAUSES THAT YOU HAVE GENERATED YESTERDAY. HOWEVER, YOU CAN INFLUENCE OR CHANGE THE COURSE OF YOUR TOMORROW BY POURING YOUR ENERGIES INTO NEW DIRECTIONS TODAY. THOUGH THE RESULTS MAY NOT COME TO PASS IMMEDIATELY, THEY MUST COME. ANY ENERGY THAT YOU GENERATE MUST HAVE AN EFFECT. A PROPER AND THOROUGH **UNDERSTANDING** OF THE LAW OF CAUSE AND EFFECT AT ALL LEVELS OF **BEING** SHALL ENABLE YOU TO ORDER YOUR LIFE SO THAT DEFINITE RESULTS SHALL ENSUE. IMAGINE A FLAT DISC ON AN INFINITE FRICTIONLESS FLAT LAKE OF ICE. THE DISC SHALL REMAIN AT REST UNTIL SOME FORCE COMPELS IT TO MOVE. ONCE IT HAS BEGUN TO MOVE, IT SHALL CONTINUE TO MOVE INDEFINITELY UNTIL SOMETHING STOPS IT. IMAGINE IF SOMEONE WERE TO EXERT A FORCE UPON THIS DISC IN ORDER TO PUSH IT IN A CERTAIN DIRECTION. AS LONG AS THIS PERSON CONTINUES

TO PUSH, THE DISC SHALL MOVE FASTER AND FASTER. HOW FAST DEPENDS UPON HOW HARD AND HOW LONG THE PERSON PUSHES IT. BECAUSE THE ICE IS FRICTIONLESS WHEN THE PERSON STOPS PUSHING, THE DISC SHALL CONTINUE TO MOVE IN THE SAME DIRECTION. THE DISC NOW HAS WITHIN IT MOMENTUM STORED FROM WHEN THE PERSON FIRST PUSHED. IT SHALL CARRY STEADILY ON IN THE DIRECTION OF THAT INITIAL PUSHING IN EXACT PROPORTION TO HOW HARD AND HOW LONG THE PERSON PUSHED. ONE SHALL HAVE TO PUSH WITH EXACTLY THE SAME AMOUNT OF FORCE IF THEY WISH TO STOP THE DISC OR GET IT MOVING IN A DIFFERENT DIRECTION. THESE LAWS WORK WITH ABSOLUTE EXACTNESS. **KNOWLEDGE** OF THESE LAWS ARE THE BASIS FOR THE CALCULATION OF FORCES WHICH LAUNCH ROCKETS INTO SPACE. **KNOWLEDGE** OF THESE LAWS ALSO ENABLE ONE TO CALCULATE EXACTLY WHAT AMOUNT OF FORCE SHALL SLOW, ACCELERATE, OR CHANGE THE DIRECTION OF AN OBJECT. THESE LAWS OF MOTION ARE PART OF THE NATURE OF THINGS BOTH PHYSICAL AND SPIRITUAL.

IN THE PRECEDING ILLUSTRATION, THE DISC REPRESENTS CONSCIOUSNESS. THE PERSON PUSHING THE DISC REPRESENTS THE WILL. THE ICE REPRESENTS LIFE. WHEN AN

INDIVIDUAL IS BORN, ITS CONSCIOUSNESS, WHICH IS ATTACHED TO A PHYSICAL BODY, BEGINS AT REST LIKE THE DISC. NO FORCE HAS YET ACTED THROUGH IT. CONSCIOUSNESS LOOKING OUT THROUGH THE SENSES OF THE BODY SEES THINGS THAT IT BELIEVES THAT IT DESIRES. THIS ACTIVATES THE WILL, WHICH THEN PROPELS A PERSON TOWARDS THEIR DESIRES BY CAUSING THEM TO WORK AND STRIVE TO OBTAIN THEM. WHATEVER A PERSON IS ATTRACTED TO, THEY STRUGGLE AND PUSH TOWARDS. IN DOING THIS, THEY BUILD AN EVER GREATER MOMENTUM IN THE DIRECTION OF THEIR DESIRES.

LIFE GIVES TO A PERSON THAT FOR WHICH THEY WORK. HOWEVER, A PROBLEM ARISES WHEN IT IS DISCOVERED THAT WHICH WAS DESIRED BRINGS SUFFERING. SOMETHING THAT WAS NOT DESIRED AT ALL. EVEN IF THE PERSON CEASES TO STRIVE TOWARDS THEIR ORIGINAL GOAL, THE MOMENTUM GAINED FROM THE INITIAL PUSH SHALL CONTINUE TO CARRY THEM IN THAT DIRECTION UNLESS AND UNTIL THEY CHOOSE A NEW DIRECTION. AFTER A LONG STRUGGLE AND CONTENTION WITH CIRCUMSTANCES, WHICH SEEM TO OPPOSE THEIR EVERY ENDEAVOR AND INTENTION TO MOVE

IN THIS NEW DIRECTION, THEY EVENTUALLY STOP THE
MOMENTUM TAKING THEM IN THE OLD DIRECTION, AND ARE
FREE TO MOVE IN THE NEW DIRECTION WHICH THEY DESIRE.
THOSE FORCES WHICH OPPOSE THEM ARE NOT MERELY THE
EQUIVALENT OF, THEY ACTUALLY ARE THE VERY SAME FORCES
THAT THEY THEMSELVES GENERATED. THE MORE THEY
STRUGGLE TO STOP THE DISC AND PUSH IT TO A NEW
DIRECTION, THE MORE VIOLENT IS THE OPPOSITION OF
THOSE FORCES OF THE PAST, BUT THE SOONER THEY ARE ABLE
TO OVERCOME THEM.

6

THEY DON'T WANT US

MAN, WHAT THE XXXX HAPPENED TO OUR CULTURE?

SOMEONE PLEASE TELL ME IF YOU KNOW,

YOU SEE, OUR CULTURE CONSISTS OF TWO ROADS,

BOTH A HIGH AND A LOW.

OUR CULTURE IS A COMPILATION OF OUR BELIEFS AND IDEAS,

FOR IT IS THEY THAT DETERMINE WHO WE ARE AND BECOME,

OUR CULTURE IS NOT THE PLACE WE CURRENTLY RESIDE,

NOR THE HOOD WE COME FROM.

OUR ORIGINAL CULTURE WAS A CULTURE OF ARISTOCRACY,

Not that of a slave,

That culture was one that was imposed upon us,

Because that's how they want us to behave.

You see, they want us to hate ourselves, LOVE

them, and sell crack to our mothers,

They want us to depend upon the system, exploit our

sisters, and murder our forgotten brothers.

They want us locked away with fifteen to life, still

thinking it's cool to do wrong,

They want us drunk and high, so we can destroy our

community, and glorify it in a song.

They want us illiterate, buried deep in our

ignorance, so no one shall ever hear us,

They want us impotent and incompetent, because

THE TRUTH is, they fear us.

They fear us because of our POWER, for we are the

founders of civilization,

This is why since birth they've bombarded us with

their diabolical indoctrination.

You see, they don't want us to know our ancestors

were kings from the most opulent land on Earth,

They don't want us to know our true culture is

MAGNIFICENCE,

FOR THEN WE MAY RECOGNIZE OUR WORTH.

YOU SEE, THEY DON'T WANT US TO KNOW ABOUT THE GREAT

MANSA MUSA,

NOR THE MOORISH EMPIRE IN SPAIN,

THEY DON'T WANT US TO KNOW OUR CULTURE IS SO MUCH

MORE THAN A SLAVE SHIP,

AND A TREMENDOUS AMOUNT OF PAIN.

THEY DON'T WANT US TO KNOW THAT KNOWLEDGE IS

THE KEY,

THAT SHALL UNLOCK THE GATES OF HEAVEN,

THEY DON'T WANT US TO KNOW THAT WE ARE AT WAR,

AND WISDOM IS OUR MOST POWERFUL WEAPON.

A MAN WHO HAS NOT FOUND SOMETHING WORTH DYING

FOR,

IS NOT FIT TO LIVE,

THEY DON'T WANT US TO KNOW THAT TO OUR CHILDREN

THE KNOWLEDGE OF SELF,

IS THE VERY BEST GIFT THAT WE CAN GIVE.

THEY DON'T WANT US TO HEAR THE WHISPERS THAT

SCREAM,

UP YOU MIGHTY RACE, YOU CAN ACCOMPLISH WHAT YOU

WILL,

THEY DON'T WANT US TO KNOW OUR TRUE PLACE IS NOT AT

THE BOTTOM,

BUT AT THE TOP OF THE HILL.

OUR CULTURE IS NOT WHAT THEY TELL US IT IS,

BUT WHAT WE DECIDE IT SHALL BE,

AND SO THE QUESTION THAT I MUST ASK YOU BROTHERS IS,

"DO YOU DESIRE TO BE A SLAVE OR FREE?"

III

FOR HE COMES OUT OF PRISON TO BE KING

Thou shalt also be a crown of glory in the hand of the LORD, and a royal diadem in the hand of thy God.

(Isaiah 62:3)

In times past, in the age when kingship was looked upon as more than a thing of myth or merely an abstract idea, when the KING had a son who had come of age and was to take the throne, the KING would send him to dwell with the very best warriors in the land so that he could be initiated. The KING did this because he who would sit on the throne had to have both the discipline and STRENGTH of a warrior. He who wore the crown had to be both willing and able to defend the kingdom from all threats. He could not afford to be weak. For if he indeed was found to be weak, the kingdom would most assuredly be lost.

In today's society, the majority of the best warriors in the land reside in three places. These three places are not the only places in the land where great warriors are found, but merely where the majority of the best are found. The first and most obvious place is in service to the martial forces of land. The armed forces, namely the military and police force. The second place where the best warriors of the land

ARE FOUND IS IN SPORTS. THIS IS MADE EVIDENT BY THE PHYSICAL AGGRESSION AND MENTAL DETERMINATION THAT ARE NECESSARY TO OBTAIN THE VICTORY THAT IS THE GOAL OF ANY ATHLETIC ENDEAVOR. JUST AS IT IS THE GOAL OF ANY MARTIAL STRUGGLE. THE THIRD PLACE WHERE THE BEST WARRIORS IN ALL OF THE LAND RESIDE IS IN THE PRISON SYSTEM. IF YOU CHOOSE TO FORGO THE CONSTRAINTS OF THE RULES OF SOCIETY IN ORDER TO BECOME ESTABLISHED IN THE CRIMINAL UNDERWORLD, IF YOU ARE NOT A WARRIOR, YOU SHALL END UP BECOMING PREY TO THOSE WHO ARE. IN THE STREETS, NOT ONLY ARE YOU AT CONSTANT WAR WITH THE ARMED FORCES OF THE POLICE, WHOSE RESOURCES ARE ENDLESS, BUT YOU MUST ALSO BE ON ALERT AGAINST THE ATTACKS AND SCHEMES COMING FROM YOUR FELLOW CRIMINALS IN THE UNDERWORLD. YOU ARE PERPETUALLY LOCKED IN A WAR OF TWO FRONTS. AS ALL WHO ARE FAMILIAR WITH THE ART OF WAR UNDERSTAND, THIS IS AN UNENVIABLE POSITION TO BE IN, TO SAY THE LEAST. THUS, IT IS THAT THE VAST MAJORITY OF WARRIORS IN THE STREET FIND THEIR CAREERS ENDING EITHER IN THE GRAVEYARD OR THE PENITENTIARY.

In my life, circumstances were arranged by my heavenly father, the supreme **KING** of the universe, for me to enter into the belly of the beast, so that I could have the opportunity to study at the feet of some of the very best warriors in all the land. At the beginning of my incarceration, one of the first things that struck me was how much prison actually reminded me of college. Of course there are some major differences between the two experiences, but there are also some major similarities as well. Ironically, it is in prison that you have more freedom to study that which you may desire to study.

In college, majors are preset in order that the system may be able to mold you into a form of its design. For example, if you major in political science, there are certain classes that you must take, certain **KNOWLEDGE** that you shall be provided with, so that you may step into a certain occupation after your graduation. An occupation that was also created by the system. You are honed into a fine-

TUNED INSTRUMENT OF THE MACHINE. **I AM** NOT SAYING THAT THERE IS ANYTHING WRONG WITH THIS, FOR INDEED THE MACHINE, LIKE EVERYTHING ELSE IN THE UNIVERSE, HAS ITS PURPOSE. **I AM** MERELY ELUCIDATING THIS TRUTH SO THAT MY POINT MAY BECOME CLEAR. ADDED TO THESE LIMITATIONS OF THE COLLEGIATE SYSTEM IS THE FACT THAT THERE ARE ONLY SO MANY MAJORS AND CLASSES THAT ARE OFFERED. THUS, THERE SHALL ALWAYS BE A LIMIT ON THE **KNOWLEDGE** THAT YOU SHALL BE ABLE TO ATTAIN THERE.

IN PRISON, HOWEVER, YOUR OPTIONS ARE LIMITLESS, PROVIDED YOU HAVE THE INITIATIVE. IF YOU HAVE THE WILL TO DO SO, YOU CAN MAJOR IN WHATSOEVER YOU DESIRE. OF COURSE, YOU SHALL NOT BE PROVIDED WITH THE VERIFICATION FOUND IN THE PIECE OF PAPER KNOWN AS A DIPLOMA, WHICH SOCIETY HAS GIVEN EXCLUSIVE CREDENCE TO IN THE CASE OF ACADEMIC ENDEAVORS, BUT YOU SHALL HAVE THE MOST IMPORTANT THING. FOR YOU SHALL HAVE OBTAINED THE **KNOWLEDGE**. A MAN CAN LITERALLY OBTAIN ANY **KNOWLEDGE** THAT HE DESIRES, AND THUS IN ESSENCE BECOME ANYTHING THAT HE WISHES.

Unfortunately, few in prison understand this truth, and thus few seize upon the opportunity to choose their major. Their major is set on default and they allow their environment to choose it for them. Many end up receiving doctorates in thievery, con artistry, gambling, laziness, and all other types of unproductive subjects. The more I pondered this, the more I began to see that these rules apply, not only in prison and college, but also in life itself. For life is the only true university, and the sooner someone selects their major, the more of an expert they shall become in their field. However, if you do not select your major consciously, one shall be thrust upon you by society. After considering my choices, I came to realize that the only major fit for me to study was kingship. And so it was that I set upon my studies with a single-pointed maniacal tenacity that appeared almost to be insanity to those observing from the outside. Thus, it was that I obtained the **KNOWLEDGE** that I now have and share with you.

1

A KING IS LOVE

(A speech given at McCormick Correctional Institution)

Peace, brothers. I come before you all today with the hope that I shall be able to adequately deliver a message unto you, which I believe shall be one of the most important messages that you shall ever receive in your life. I humbly stand before you, brothers, on this day in order to speak to you on the Kwanzaa principle of Nia, which stands for purpose. A man that has no purpose in life, is like a man who sets out on a journey, but has no idea where he is going, or what direction he shall take to get there. Now, obviously, a man such as this shall get nowhere and accomplish nothing. For until a man unites his mind with purpose, there shall be no achievement except for aimlessness, which only leads one to catastrophe, disaster, and destruction. Three places that no sane man would ever choose to venture.

Those who have no purpose in life easily fall victim

TO PETTINESS, FEAR, SELF-PITY, AND DESPAIR. FOR THEIR MINDS HAVE NOT THE **STRENGTH** THAT IS GIVEN BY PURPOSE TO RESIST THESE GREAT DESTROYERS OF ASPIRATION. THOSE THAT ARE WISE KNOW THAT THE ROAD TO SELF-CONTROL AND CONCENTRATION, THE VERY ROAD TO GREATNESS, BEGINS WITH THE CONCEIVING OF A PURPOSE IN ONE'S HEART. CONTINUES WITH THE MAKING OF THIS PURPOSE THE CENTRALIZING POINT IN ONE'S THOUGHTS. AND ENDS IN THE MAKING OF THIS PURPOSE ONE'S SUPREME DUTY.

BROTHERS, EACH AND EVERY ONE OF US BEGAN OUR PHYSICAL EXISTENCE IN THIS WORLD AS A SINGLE SPERM CELL LIVING AMONGST MOST HUNDREDS OF MILLIONS IN THE TESTICLES OF OUR FATHERS. EACH AND EVERY ONE OF US WERE THEN SENT FORTH ON THE MOST DANGEROUS AND IMPORTANT MISSION THAT YOU CAN IMAGINE. FOR WE WERE SENT FORTH ON THE MISSION OF REACHING OUR MOTHER'S EGG, AND FERTILIZING IT IN ORDER TO ATTAIN LIFE. TO FAIL IN THIS MISSION MEANT DEATH AND WE KNEW IT. AND SO DID THE MILLIONS OF OTHERS WHO SET OUT ON THIS GREAT QUEST ALONG WITH US. FOR EXCEPT IN

THE RARE MIRACLE OF TWINS, ONLY ONE OUT OF THE
MILLIONS THAT WERE SENT FORTH WOULD SUCCEED IN THIS
MISSION. ONLY ONE. OUT OF THE MILLIONS THAT WERE
SENT FORTH, ONLY ONE HAD THE SUPREME INTELLIGENCE
AND THE SUPREME WILLPOWER THAT WERE NECESSARY TO
SUCCEED. ONLY ONE. NOW THINK ABOUT THAT FOR A
SECOND. I MEAN REALLY THINK ABOUT IT. WHERE
MILLIONS FAILED, YOU WERE THE ONLY ONE IN POSSESSION
OF WHAT IT TOOK TO SUCCEED.

OUT OF MILLIONS, BROTHERS, WE WERE THE ONES WHO
WERE PREEMINENT. WE WERE THE ONES WHO REIGNED
SUPREME. SO YOU SEE, BEFORE OUR MOTHERS NAMED US,
BEFORE THEY WERE EVEN FULLY AWARE OF OUR EXISTENCE, WE
EARNED, AND THUS GOD BESTOWED UPON US THE TITLE OF
KING. KINGS! THIS IS WHO WE ARE. THIS IS WHAT WE
MUST BECOME. FOR THIS IS OUR PURPOSE. THE SLAIN
PROPHET, MALCOLM X, ONCE STATED, "IN FACT, PRISON
ENABLED ME TO STUDY FAR MORE INTENSIVELY THAN I
WOULD HAVE IF MY LIFE HAD GONE DIFFERENTLY AND I HAD
ATTENDED SOME COLLEGE."[4] BEFORE HIM ANOTHER GREAT

---

[4] X, Malcolm. 1988. *The Autobiography of Malcolm X.*

MAN ONCE SAID, "IF A MAN TREATS PRISON LIKE A UNIVERSITY, HE SHALL WALK OUT A KING."[5] KING SOLOMON, THE SON OF DAVID, KING OF ISRAEL WROTE IN THE BOOK OF ECCLESIASTES, "BETTER A POOR AND WISE YOUTH THAN AN OLD AND FOOLISH KING WHO WILL BE ADMONISHED NO MORE. FOR HE COMES OUT OF PRISON TO BE KING, ALTHOUGH HE WAS BORN POOR IN HIS KINGDOM" (4:13-14, NKJV). HOW MANY OF YOU WERE BORN POOR IN YOUR KINGDOM? AS YOU BELIEVE, SO SHALL YOU ACT. AS YOU ACT, SO SHALL GO YOUR DESTINY. YOU SEE, IN ORDER TO TRULY BE A KING, YOU MUST FIRST BELIEVE THAT YOU ARE A KING. IN ORDER TO COME TO BELIEVE THAT YOU ARE A KING, YOU MUST GAIN THE KNOWLEDGE OF A KING. THE FIRST KNOWLEDGE OF A KING THAT YOU MUST GAIN IS THE KNOWLEDGE OF THE DUTY OF A KING. IT IS THE DUTY OF A KING TO BE A MIRROR TO HIS PEOPLE OF THE GREATNESS WHICH LIES WITHIN THEMSELVES. FOR HOW COULD A PERSON KNOW THAT THEY ARE BEAUTIFUL IF THEY NEVER SEE A BEAUTIFUL REFLECTION OF THEMSELVES? IT IS ALSO A KING'S DUTY TO UNITE HIS PEOPLE IN HARMONY.

---

[5] Author Unknown.

For a kingdom divided against itself shall never be able to stand. However, to accomplish both of these things, it is only necessary that a **KING** fulfills his supreme and most paramount duty which is to be a manifestation of **DIVINE LOVE**, the **LOVE** of God upon the Earth. In order to become a manifestation of **LOVE**, one must manifest the attributes of **LOVE**.

Thus, **A KING IS PATIENT**

A **KING** understands that a patient heart is a fertile field for life's greatest miracles. Contrary to popular belief, patience produces immediate results, with the most important of these results being peace of mind, with which all may be accomplished. Time is the most valuable weapon that a **KING** possesses. For if he would patiently keep in mind any long term goal, there is nary person, nor army on Earth that shall be able to resist him. Even the greatest of castles, and the most glorious of kingdoms, began with the laying of a single stone. Almighty patience is the supreme virtue of the powerful, while

IMPATIENCE ONLY SERVES TO MAKE ONE APPEAR WEAK. FOR THOSE WHO ARE IMPATIENT OVERESTIMATE WHAT CAN BE DONE IN A SHORT AMOUNT OF TIME, BUT UNDERESTIMATE WHAT CAN BE ACCOMPLISHED OVER A LONG PERIOD OF TIME. A **KING** UNDERSTANDS THAT TIME SHALL ALWAYS BE THE ALLY OF HE WHO WORSHIPS **DIVINE** PATIENCE.

A KING IS KIND

IT IS THE WEAK WHO ARE CRUEL. GENTLENESS AND MERCY CAN ONLY BE EXPECTED FROM THOSE WHO ARE STRONG. A **KING** IS KIND, BECAUSE THOSE WHO WALK THE PATH OF TRUE GREATNESS ARE ALWAYS ACCOMPANIED BY KINDNESS. IT IS A MARK OF GREAT **WISDOM** IN A MAN WHEN HE DISPLAYS SKILL IN WINNING THE FRIENDLY COOPERATION OF OTHERS. FOR HARMONIOUS COOPERATION IS A PRICELESS ASSET THAT SHALL ONLY BE ACQUIRED IN PROPORTION TO THE AMOUNT THAT IS GIVEN. WHAT HEAT IS TO BUTTER, KINDNESS IS TO HUMAN NATURE. FRIENDLY COUNSEL SHALL CARRY MORE WEIGHT AND HAVE MORE **POWER** TO INFLUENCE THAN UNFRIENDLY CRITICISM EVER SHALL. A **KING** UNDERSTANDS THAT HE WHO HAS AN AGREEABLE AND KIND PERSONALITY POSSESSES THE **POWER** TO COMPEL

ALMOST ANYONE TO BEHAVE TOWARDS HIM AS HE WISHES THEM TO BEHAVE. FOR KIND PERSUASION SHALL ALWAYS BE MORE EFFECTIVE THAN MALICIOUS FORCE.

A KING DOES NOT ENVY

A **KING** UNDERSTANDS THAT WHOSOEVER CONTRACTS THE DISEASE OF ENVY POISONS THEIR OWN SOUL. THE ENVIOUS ARE MERELY FOOLS WHO ARE FOOLISH ENOUGH TO ACCUSE THE GREAT OF BEING INFERIOR BECAUSE OF THEIR GREATNESS. THE MAN WHO ENVIES HAS THE EXTREME MISFORTUNE OF DYING NOT ONLY ONCE, BUT AS MANY TIMES AS THE PERSON WHOM HE ENVIES, HEARS THE SWEET VOICE OF PRAISE. A **KING** UNDERSTANDS THAT WHEREVER ENVY IS ALLOWED TO RULE UNCHECKED, WAR AND DISASTER MUST NECESSARILY FOLLOW. JUST AS RUST CAN SILENTLY DESTROY THE STRONGEST AND STURDIEST SWORD, SO TOO CAN ENVY SILENTLY CORRUPT AND CONTAMINATE THE STOUTEST OF HEARTS IF IT IS ALLOWED TO ENTER.

A KING DOES NOT BOAST

IT IS ONLY THE INSECURE WHO FEEL THE NEED TO BOAST AND FLAUNT THEIR VICTORIES OVER OTHERS. THOSE WHO ARE TRULY POWERFUL KNOW THAT THE APPEARANCE OF SUPERIORITY OVER OTHERS IS TRIVIAL COMPARED TO THE REALITY OF IT. A GREAT **KING** NEVER TAKES PLEASURE OUT OF MAKING OTHERS FEEL INFERIOR. A **KING** UNDERSTANDS IT IS ALWAYS BEST TO TALK LESS ABOUT ONE'S OWN ACHIEVEMENTS THAN IT IS TO DISCUSS THE ACHIEVEMENTS OF OTHERS. FOR MODESTY SHALL ALWAYS BE PREFERABLE TO ARROGANCE, AND IT IS BY EXPRESSING MODEST ADMIRATION FOR THE ACHIEVEMENTS OF OTHERS THAT ONE BRINGS ATTENTION TO ONE'S OWN. A TRUE **KING** CONVINCES OTHERS THAT HE IS **KING**, NOT BY HIS SPEECH, BUT BY HIS PRESENCE. HE UNDERSTANDS THAT RESPECT MUST BE EARNED WITH DEEDS, NOT WORDS. A **KING** DOES NOT BOAST, FOR A **KING** KNOWS THAT TRUE NOBILITY IS NOT FOUND IN BEING BETTER THAN SOMEONE ELSE, BUT RATHER IN BEING BETTER THAN ONE USED TO BE.

A KING IS NOT ARROGANT

Arrogance, a sign of insecurity, is the polar opposite of a royal demeanor. Thus, the thrones of the arrogant are soon overturned. For those whom the **DIVINE** would destroy It first makes arrogant. A **KING** always seeks to radiate confidence, but at all cost he shuns any show of arrogance. For to invite hatred without any resulting advantage is not only unwise, but vain as well. The greater he is, the more a **KING** must humble himself. For if he conducts all of his affairs with humility, a **KING** shall be loved more than a giver of gifts. A universal characteristic of greatness is humility. For those who are truly great understand that, not only do their abilities come from a higher influence, but also that if they humble not themselves, life shall arrange to have them humbled. For all who exalt themselves shall be humbled, and all who humble themselves shall be exalted. A great **KING** is always willing to be little. For humility of heart shall attract more sincere friendships than all the riches of the world.

A KING IS NOT ARROGANT, BECAUSE A KING UNDERSTANDS THAT NO MATTER HOW GREAT HIS TALENTS AND INTELLECTUAL ACHIEVEMENTS, THEY ARE AS NOTHING IN THE FACE OF THE ETERNAL.

A KING IS NOT RUDE

A KING UNDERSTANDS THAT THE GREATER HIS COURTESY, THE GREATER SHALL BE HIS RENOWN, HIS FAME, AND HIS GLORY. THEREFORE, A KING ALWAYS MEASURES THE WORDS THAT HE WOULD CHOOSE TO USE WITH THE YARDSTICK OF COURTESY. THERE IS NEVER AN EXCUSE FOR THE CARELESS USE OF WORDS THAT MAY OFFEND OTHERS. A KING KNOWS THAT ONE WORD THOUGHTLESSLY SPOKEN, JUST ONE, IS ABLE TO DESTROY THE HAPPINESS OF A LIFETIME. IF ONE WOULD BUT GUARD HIS WORDS, HIS WORDS SHALL FOREVER GUARD HIM IN RETURN. THERE IS NEVER ANYTHING TO BE GAINED FROM UNNECESSARILY INSULTING ANYONE. FOR ONE CAN NEVER BE COMPLETELY SURE WHO ONE IS DEALING WITH SHALL BECOME IN THE FUTURE.

A TRUE KING ALWAYS MURDERS HIS IMPULSE TO OFFEND, EVEN IF THE OTHER PERSON IS AN ENEMY AND DESERVING OF

OFFENCE. FOR THE SATISFACTION GAINED FROM INSULTING IS A TRIFLING THING COMPARED TO THE THREAT OF REVENGE. IN FACT, TO ABSTAIN FROM INJURIOUS AND INSULTING LANGUAGE IS ONE OF THE WISEST PRECAUTIONS THAT A **KING** CAN TAKE WHEN FACING AN ENEMY. FOR INSULTS, WHILE TAKING NOTHING FROM THE **STRENGTH** OF AN ADVERSARY, RAISES THEIR HATRED TO THE POINT WHERE THEY CONTEMPLATE NOTHING MORE DILIGENTLY THAN THE DESTRUCTION OF THE ONE FROM WHOM THEY RECEIVED THE INSULT.

THERE IS GREAT **POWER** IN COURTESY. FOR COURTESY IS AN IRRESISTIBLE FORCE WITH WHICH ONE MAY DISARM ALL ENEMIES AND AN ANTAGONIST. NO, BROTHERS. A **KING** IS NOT RUDE. FOR A **KING** UNDERSTANDS THAT THOSE WHO MANIFEST HATE OR DISRESPECT TOWARDS OTHERS DO SO, BECAUSE HATE AND A LACK OF RESPECT ARE FELT AT A DEEPER LEVEL TOWARDS THEMSELVES.

A KING IS NOT SELF-SEEKING

A **KING** IS NOT SELF-SEEKING, BECAUSE A **KING** DOES NOT RULE TO BE SERVED. ON THE CONTRARY, A **KING**

RULES SO THAT HE MAY BE A SERVANT TO HIS PEOPLE, AND SO THAT HE MAY HAVE THE PRIVILEGE OF GIVING HIS LIFE TO HIS KINGDOM. A **KING** UNDERSTANDS THAT WHAT HE DOES FOR HIMSELF ALONE SHALL DIE WITH HIM, BUT WHAT HE DOES FOR HIS KINGDOM SHALL NEVER DIE. IT IS THE COMMON MAN WHO SEEKS SOLACE IN SELFISHNESS, WHILE THE QUESTION THAT A **KING** ASKS HIMSELF ON A DAILY BASIS IS, "WHAT CAN I DO FOR OTHERS WITH THE **POWER** THAT I HAVE?" A **KING** RECOGNIZES THE ADVANTAGES OF SERVING. HE UNDERSTANDS THAT WHEN HE REACHES BEYOND HIMSELF TO CARE FOR ANOTHER, HE IS LED PAST HIS OWN FEARS AND LIMITATIONS. HE WHO RENDERS THE GREATEST SERVICE TO OTHERS, UNCOVERS THE GREATEST OPPORTUNITY OF BENEFIT FOR HIMSELF. FOR ONE SHALL ALWAYS EVENTUALLY BE REWARDED FOR ACTIONS THAT REVEAL A SENSE OF SELF-SACRIFICE AND DEVOTION. ALTHOUGH SERVICE IS THE RENT THAT ONE MUST PAY FOR THE PRIVILEGE OF BEING **KING**, A **KING** UNDERSTANDS THAT IF HE WOULD SERVE DILIGENTLY, HE HIMSELF SHALL BE SERVED IN RETURN. FOR THOSE WHO DO NOT PUT THEMSELVES AND THEIR OWN INTEREST FIRST ARE TRULY RARE. AND THAT WHICH IS RARE IS ALWAYS VALUABLE. HE

WHO IS A TRUE **KING** SHALL ALWAYS PLACE THE NATION ABOVE THE CROWN AND THE COMMUNITY ABOVE HIMSELF. ABSENT THIS EMPATHY, ANY **KING**, EVEN ONE THAT WAS ONCE WISE, SHALL PROVE TO BE NO LONGER A **KING**, BUT A TYRANT.

A KING IS NOT EASILY ANGERED

A **KING** IS NOT EASILY ANGERED, FOR A **KING** UNDERSTANDS THAT ANGER IS A TRAITOR THAT ONLY SERVES TO LIMIT ONE'S OPTIONS. THIS IS THE GREATEST FOLLY THAT ANY **KING** COULD EVER COMMIT. FOR THE LIMITING OF ONE'S OPTIONS ULTIMATELY LIMITS ONE'S **POWER**, WHICH IS THE VERY OPPOSITE OF WHAT A **KING** OUGHT TO DESIRE. TO SHOW FRUSTRATION, OR PETULANCE, IS NOT A SIGN OF **STRENGTH** AS THE COMMON MAN BELIEVES, BUT A SIGN OF IMPOTENCE. FOR TO DISPLAY THESE CHARACTERISTICS IS TO SHOW THE WORLD THAT ONE HAS LOST THE **POWER** TO SHAPE EVENTS WITH ONE'S WILL. A TRUE **KING** WOULD NEVER REVEAL THIS KIND OF WEAKNESS. FOR THIS IS THE ACTION OF A HELPLESS CHILD WHO MUST THROW A TANTRUM TO GET HIS WAY. HE WHO POSSESSES SUCH LITTLE SELF-CONTROL THAT HE WOULD

THROW A TANTRUM IS NOT WORTHY OF A THRONE. EVEN
IN THE FACE OF THE RUDENESS OF OTHERS, A **KING**
ALWAYS KEEPS POSSESSION OF HIS SERENITY. FOR HE
UNDERSTANDS THAT TO REACT CONSTANTLY TO THE
ACTIONS OF ANOTHER IS TO GIVE THAT PERSON CONTROL
OVER HIM AND HIS KINGDOM. FOR THE MOOD INTO
WHICH A PERSON IS ABLE TO BRING YOU IS IN DIRECT
CORRELATION TO THAT PERSON'S DOMINION OVER YOU.
ALTHOUGH HE MAY NOT BE ABLE TO CONTROL THE ACTIONS
OF OTHERS, A **KING** MUST ALWAYS CONTROL HIS MENTAL
REACTION TO THEIR ACTS. FOR THIS IS WHAT SHALL SHAPE
HIS REALITY. LIKE A SHEEP WITHOUT A SHEPHERD, THOSE
WHO ARE EASILY ANGERED ARE EASILY LED ASTRAY. FOR THE
LESS CALM ONE IS, THE LESS ALERT ONE IS. AND IT IS THOSE
EMOTIONS WHICH PEOPLE ARE THE LEAST ABLE TO CONTROL
THAT ARE THE ONES BY WHICH THEY MAY BE THE MOST
EASILY CONTROLLED. IT IS BY SHOWING A CALM, UNRUFFLED
EXTERIOR IN THE FACE OF UNPLEASANTNESS THAT A **KING**
IS ABLE TO PUT HIS PEOPLE AT EASE. THEREFORE, IT IS
CRUCIAL THAT A **KING** MAINTAINS THE ABILITY TO ADAPT
HIMSELF TO ALL CHANGING CIRCUMSTANCES AND
AFFLICTIONS WITHOUT LOSING HIS SENSE OF COMPOSURE.

FOR HE WHO IS UNABLE TO DO SO, IS UNFIT FOR THE THRONE.

A KING KEEPS NO RECORD OF WRONGS

A **KING** KEEPS NO RECORD OF WRONGS, BECAUSE TO DO SO WOULD LEAD TO RESENTMENT, AND A **KING** UNDERSTANDS THAT RESENTMENT IS AN EMOTION THAT SHALL NAIL HIM TO THE CROSS OF HIS OWN RUINED PAST. HE WHO HOLDS ONTO RESENTMENTS BECOMES VENGEFUL, AND THUS ATTACHED TO, AND DEPENDENT UPON THE VERY PEOPLE WHO HAVE CAUSED HIM PAIN. THE VENGEFUL BELIEVE THAT THE ONLY WAY THEY CAN BE RELEASED FROM THE PAIN THAT THEY FEEL IS BY HARMING THOSE THAT THEY BELIEVE HAVE MADE THEM SUFFER. THE ONLY PEOPLE THAT A **KING** MUST SEEK TO GET EVEN WITH ARE THOSE THAT HAVE HELPED HIM ALONG HIS PATH TO GREATNESS. THE ONLY WAY ONE SHALL BECOME GREAT IS IF THEY HAVE THE **STRENGTH** OF WILL NECESSARY TO UNDERGO INCONVENIENCES AND ENDURE INSULTS WITHOUT RESENTMENT. A **KING** UNDERSTANDS THAT WHATEVER ONE MAKES A HABIT OF LOOKING FOR IN OTHERS, ONE

EVENTUALLY FINDS MIRRORED IN ONE'S OWN CHARACTER.
THEREFORE, THE HABIT OF LOOKING FOR WRONGS TO
RECORD IN OTHERS EVENTUALLY LEADS TO THE DEVELOPMENT
OF WRONG IN ONESELF.

A KING DOES NOT DELIGHT IN EVIL

EVIL IS IGNORANCE, AND IGNORANCE IS EVIL. THUS, THOSE
THAT DELIGHT IN IGNORANCE ARE WICKED, FOR ONLY THE
WICKED WOULD TAKE DELIGHT IN THEIR IGNORANCE.
ALTHOUGH THERE SHALL BE TIMES WHEN EVIL IS ABLE TO
EXERT ITS **POWER** BY MAKING THE DARKNESS OF
IGNORANCE APPEAR TO BE THE LIGHT OF **WISDOM**, EVIL
SHALL ALWAYS BOW BEFORE THE GOOD, AND THE WICKED
BEFORE THE RIGHTEOUS. A **KING** UNDERSTANDS THAT
WHEREAS GOOD KINGS RULE NOT FOR THEMSELVES BUT FOR
THEIR PEOPLE, EVIL KINGS GO IN FEAR OF THE VERY PEOPLE
THAT THEY RULE. THE MORE **POWER** THEY POSSESS, THE
MORE ENEMIES THEY SHALL HAVE. FOR THE GREATER THE
POWER THE IGNORANCE ENJOYS, THE MORE HARM IT
SHALL BE ABLE TO DO. A WISE **KING** UNDERSTANDS THAT
PAIN FOLLOWS EVIL THOUGHTS, JUST AS WETNESS FOLLOWS

THE RAIN. THEREFORE, HE WOULD NEVER DELIGHT IN EVIL, FOR HE KNOWS THAT IF A MAN WOULD BANISH WEAK EVIL THOUGHTS FROM HIS MIND AND THINK ONLY GOOD STRONG THOUGHTS, THE WORLD ITSELF WOULD SOFTEN TOWARDS HIM, AND BE EVER READY TO HELP HIM. INDEED, OPPORTUNITY SHALL SPRING UP AT EVERY TURN TO AID THE **KING** WHO REFUSES TO DELIGHT IN EVIL, AND NO CIRCUMSTANCE SHALL EVER BE ABLE TO BIND HIM TO SHAME.

A KING REJOICES WITH THE TRUTH

A **KING** SHALL ALWAYS REJOICE WITH **THE TRUTH**. FOR A **KING** UNDERSTANDS THAT ACCEPTING **THE TRUTH** IS THE FIRST STEP IN GAINING CONTROL OF HIS DESTINY. HE WHO REFUSES TO ACCEPT **THE TRUTH** SHALL BE ASSASSINATED BY LIES. HARMONY IS **THE TRUTH** OF THE UNIVERSE. THUS, IT IS ONLY BY KNOWING AND LIVING **THE TRUTH** THAT A **KING** IS ABLE TO BECOME A SOURCE OF HARMONY TO ALL. A **KING** NEVER FEARS **THE TRUTH**. FOR A **KING** KNOWS THAT MERCY AND **THE TRUTH** SHALL ALWAYS PRESERVE HIM AS LONG AS HE UPHOLDS HIS THRONE WITH COMPASSION. IT IS **THE TRUTH** THAT GIVES A **KING** THE ABILITY TO BE

HIS OWN MAN. FOR EVEN AMONGST A CROWD OF LIES, **THE TRUTH** HAS THE **STRENGTH** TO STAND ALONE. BECAUSE A **KING** KNOWS BETTER THAN TO MISTAKE HIS EDUCATION FOR **KNOWLEDGE** OF REALITY ITSELF, HE ALWAYS REMAINS OPEN TO HEARING **THE TRUTH**. WHILE IT SHALL FOREVER REMAIN TO THE GLORY OF THE UNIVERSE TO CONCEAL **THE TRUTH**, IT IS TO THE GLORY OF A **KING** TO DISCOVER IT. A TRUE **KING** ALWAYS LOVES AND SHOWS PREFERENCE TO THOSE WHO SPEAK **THE TRUTH**. GOSSIP, RUMORS, AND OPINIONS ARE FRIVOLOUS, PLENTIFUL, AND FREE. FACTS AND TRUTH, HOWEVER, ARE RARE AND PRECIOUS JEWELS. FOR THEIR PRICE IS THE METICULOUS LABOR THAT IS NECESSARY TO EXAMINE THEM FOR ACCURACY. A **KING** UNDERSTANDS THAT ALTHOUGH THE FATE OF HIS KINGDOM RESTS FOREVER PRECARIOUSLY BALANCED UPON THE EDGE OF A KNIFE, **THE TRUTH** SHALL KEEP HIM FOREVER UPRIGHT. FOR GREATNESS OCCURS WHEN ONE IS ABLE TO SEE A SIMPLE TRUTH BEHIND A TANGLE OF COMPLICATED LIES.

A KING ALWAYS PROTECTS

A KING ALWAYS PROTECTS, BECAUSE HE WHO DOES NOT PROTECT HIS PEOPLE IS NO KING AT ALL. THUS, IT IS CRUCIAL THAT A KING BE A WARRIOR ALSO. FOR INDEED HE SHALL HAVE TO FIGHT FOR THE SECURITY OF HIS KINGDOM, BATTLING BOTH ASSAULT FROM WITHOUT, AND MUTINY FROM WITHIN. A KING DELIGHTS IN PROTECTING THOSE WHO ARE UNABLE TO PROTECT THEMSELVES. FOR A KING UNDERSTANDS THAT TO SOOTHE A PERSON'S FEARS BY PROVIDING THEM SECURITY IN THEIR TIME OF DISTRESS IS TO GAIN AN ALLY IN ONE'S OWN TIME OF DISTRESS. A KING ALWAYS PROTECTS, FOR A KING KNOWS THAT IF HE CAN FIND NO WAY TO PROTECT HIS KINGDOM, THERE IS NONE THAT SHALL.

A KING ALWAYS TRUSTS

TRUST IS FAITH AND FAITH IS TRUST. A KING ALWAYS TRUSTS, BECAUSE FAITH IS THE FOUNDATION OF HARMONY, AND LOVE IS NOTHING WITHOUT TRUST. A KING NEVER FEARS TO TRUST, FOR A KING UNDERSTANDS THAT IF HE WOULD JUST PAY ATTENTION,

THAT GREAT INSTRUCTOR OF **WISDOM** WHICH MEN CALL EXPERIENCE, SHALL ALWAYS SHOW HIM WHOM HE MAY TRUST. ONE PERSON THAT A **KING** MUST ALWAYS HAVE TRUST IN IS HIMSELF. FOR NOT ONLY IS IT IMPOSSIBLE FOR A MAN WITH NO **FAITH** IN HIMSELF TO BE SINCERE IN HIS DEALINGS WITH OTHERS, BUT HE WHO TRUSTS NOT HIMSELF CAN NEVER RELY UPON HIMSELF, AND THUS SHALL NEVER SUCCEED. SELF-RELIANCE IS THE TOOL WHICH DEFEATS ALL OPPOSITION AND OVERCOMES ALL OBSTACLES. A **KING** ALWAYS TRUSTS. FOR A **KING** UNDERSTANDS THAT HE WHO CAN NEVER TRUST COMPLETELY, CAN NEVER BE COMPLETELY TRUSTED.

A KING ALWAYS HOPES

A **KING** ALWAYS HOPES, FOR HE WHO IS WISE KNOWS THAT ONE CAN NEVER BE SURE OF THE FINAL PICTURE UNTIL ALL OF THE PIECES OF THE PUZZLE FALL INTO PLACE. A **KING** UNDERSTANDS THAT NO MATTER HOW BLEAK THINGS MAY SEEM, IT IS IMPERATIVE THAT HE NEVER LOSES HOPE. FOR SINCE HE KNOWS NOT WHAT HIS END IS GOING TO BE, BUT IS STEADILY TRAVELING TOWARDS THAT END IN DARKNESS,

AND ON UNTRAVELED PATHS, HE MUST ALWAYS RELY UPON HOPE AS HIS GUIDE AND NEVER ABANDON THIS GUIDE, AND NEVER ALLOW IT TO ABANDON HIM, NO MATTER WHAT MAY BEFALL HIM. EVEN IN THE FACE OF CERTAIN DEATH, A TRUE **KING** SHALL ALWAYS SEE THE FACE OF HOPE. FOR A TRUE **KING** UNDERSTANDS THAT THE FULL EXTENT OF ALL HUMAN **WISDOM** IS CONTAINED IN THE TWO WORDS, WAIT AND HOPE.

A KING ALWAYS PERSEVERES

A NOBLE HEART CAN ALWAYS BE FOUND IN THE MAN WHO PERSEVERES. MISFORTUNE AND HUMILIATION MERELY SERVE TO PURIFY A MAN AND PROVE HIS WORTH. A **KING** UNDERSTANDS THAT ADVERSITY IS A TOOL WHICH HE MAY USE IN ORDER TO ATTAIN SUCCESS. FOR IF HE SEES AND ACCEPTS ADVERSITY AS INSPIRATION FOR GREATER EFFORT AND DETERMINATION, HIS **FAITH** SHALL BECOME SO POWERFUL THAT IT SHALL DESTROY ALL OBSTACLES IN HIS PATH. IN FACT, BECAUSE A **KING** ONLY BECOMES GREAT WHEN HE OVERCOMES THE DIFFICULTIES AND HINDRANCES BY WHICH HE IS CONFRONTED, FATE, WHENEVER SHE DESIRES

TO MAKE A **KING** GREAT, CONSTRUCTS IMPEDIMENTS AGAINST HIM IN ORDER TO GIVE HIM THE OPPORTUNITY TO OVERCOME THEM, AND USE THEM AS THE STEPPING STONES WHICH SHALL ALLOW HIM TO CLIMB TO THE HEIGHTS OF GREATNESS.

THE WISE **KING** DOES NOT RECOGNIZE OBSTACLES AS ANYTHING BESIDES THE BUILDING BLOCKS OF OPPORTUNITY WEARING A CLEVER DISGUISE. ADVERSITY TEACHES LESSONS THAT CAN ONLY BE LEARNED BY GOING THROUGH ADVERSITY. HARDSHIP, IF A **KING** ALLOWS IT TO, SHALL REVEAL **POWER** TO HIM THAT HE NEVER KNEW HE POSSESSED. A **KING** KNOWS THAT IF ONE FINDS THEMSELVES IN A DESPERATE PLACE, AND IT SEEMS THAT THEY COULD NOT HOLD ON FOR ONE SECOND LONGER, IT IS THEN THAT THEY MUST MURDER THE URGE TO GIVE UP. FOR THIS IS EXACTLY THE TIME WHEN FORTUNE SHALL TURN IN THEIR FAVOR. FOR FORTUNE SHALL ALWAYS TURN IN A MAN'S FAVOR IF HE'S DETERMINED TO SEE THAT IT DOES. LIFE IS SO DESIGNED THAT EVERY MAN WHO SHALL ACHIEVE GREAT SUCCESS MUST FIRST UNDERGO A PERIOD OF AFFLICTIONS, SOMETIMES MANY OF THEM, THROUGH WHICH HE SHALL BE

EXAMINED FOR DETERMINATION AND COURAGE. HE WHO QUITS WHEN ADVERSITY OVERTAKES HIM CONFESSES TO THE ENTIRE UNIVERSE THAT HE MISTOOK HIS VANITY FOR TRUE CONFIDENCE. ALL ADVERSITIES EXIST FOR THE SAKE OF MAKING DEMANDS UPON A **KING** TO REACH INTO THE DEPTHS OF HIS SPIRIT TO AWAKEN THE **POWER** NECESSARY TO OVERCOME THEM. FOR SINCE NO ONE IS ABLE TO EXERT FORCE WITHOUT OPPOSITION, THERE CAN BE NO MANIFESTATION OF **POWER** WITHOUT ADVERSITY.

Finally brothers, **A KING MUST HAVE A VISION**

A **KING** MUST HAVE A VISION OF THE PERFECTION WHICH HE SEEKS FOR BOTH HIMSELF AND HIS KINGDOM. WHEN A **KING** HAS NO VISION, HIS KINGDOM SHALL PERISH. THEREFORE, THE MOST IMPORTANT THING THAT A **KING** MUST POSSESS IS A VISION. FOR A MAN'S ABILITY TO HAVE A VISION IS WHAT MAKES HIM **DIVINE**. IF HE REMAINS FOCUSED UPON HIS VISION, A **KING** SHALL TOUCH THE FRINGES OF ETERNITY DURING HIS LIFE. FOR VISIONS ARE MAN'S LINK TO IMMORTALITY. FOR GREATNESS TO BE ACHIEVED, A **KING** MUST AT ALL TIMES KEEP HIS VISION IN THE FORE OF HIS MIND, AND IN EVERY SITUATION, SEEK THE

HIGHEST OUTCOME ACCORDING TO THAT VISION. FOR ATTAINING HIS HIGHEST VISION AND BECOMING HIS IDEAL SELF COMES DOWN TO A SERIES OF CHOICES A **KING** MUST MAKE ON A DAILY BASIS IN WHICH, TIME AND TIME AGAIN, HE REFUSES TO CHOOSE THAT WHICH IS BENEATH HIS IDEAL.

IF A **KING** CONTINUALLY REFUSES TO CHOOSE THE LESS THAN IDEAL VISION, THE LESS THAN IDEAL MOTIVATION, THE LESS THAN IDEAL SOLUTION, AND THE LESS THAN IDEAL GOAL, AND INSTEAD CHOOSES TO PATIENTLY AWAIT THE COMING OF HIS HIGHEST IDEALS, THE UNIVERSE SHALL ALWAYS REWARD HIS PATIENCE AND TRUST WITH MAGNIFICENCE. A MAN SHALL NEVER TRULY BECOME A **KING** UNTIL HE POSSESSES AND PURSUES A VISION. FOR IT IS ONLY ON THE PATH TO ACTUALIZING ONE'S VISION THAT ONE SHALL ACQUIRE THE **WISDOM** AND **STRENGTH** NECESSARY TO RULE.

IT IS AT THIS TIME THAT I MUST IMPLORE ALL OF THE KINGS OF THE WORLD TO PLEASE ARISE. PLEASE STAND IF YOU ARE ABLE TO, FOR THE WORLD NEEDS TO KNOW WHO YOU ARE. MY BROTHERS. MY FELLOW KINGS. I MUST FINISH MY

MESSAGE TO YOU BY ISSUING UNTO YOU THIS DIRE WARNING.
IF YOU HAVE TAKEN HEED OF NOTHING ELSE THAT I HAVE
SAID TODAY, I BESEECH YOU TO TAKE HEED OF THIS. IF YOU
DO NOT BECOME THE **KING** THAT YOU WERE DESTINED TO
BE, YOU SHALL BECOME THE SLAVE THAT THE ENEMY DESIRES
YOU TO BECOME. RESPECT.

2

AND THE LORD APPEARED TO SOLOMON AT GIBEON. HE
SPOKE TO HIM IN A DREAM DURING THE NIGHT. GOD SAID,
"ASK FOR ANYTHING YOU WANT ME TO GIVE YOU."
SOLOMON ANSWERED, "YOU HAVE BEEN VERY KIND TO MY
FATHER DAVID, YOUR SERVANT. THAT IS BECAUSE HE WAS
FAITHFUL TO YOU. HE DID WHAT WAS RIGHT. HIS HEART
WAS HONEST. AND YOU HAVE CONTINUED TO BE VERY KIND
TO HIM. YOU HAVE GIVEN HIM A SON TO SIT ON HIS
THRONE THIS DAY. LORD MY GOD, YOU HAVE MADE ME
KING. YOU HAVE PUT ME IN THE PLACE OF MY FATHER
DAVID. BUT I AM ONLY A LITTLE CHILD. I DON'T KNOW
HOW TO CARRY OUT MY DUTIES. I AM HERE AMONG THE
PEOPLE THAT YOU HAVE CHOSEN. THEY ARE A GREAT

NATION. THEY ARE MORE THAN ANYONE CAN COUNT. SO GIVE ME A HEART THAT UNDERSTANDS. THEN I CAN RULE OVER YOUR PEOPLE. THEN I SHALL HAVE THE WISDOM TO TELL THE DIFFERENCE BETWEEN WHAT IS RIGHT AND WHAT IS WRONG. WHO CAN POSSIBLY RULE OVER THIS GREAT NATION OF YOURS?" (1 KINGS 3:5-9).

UNDERSTANDING IS THE ONE THING THAT ALL KINGS MUST POSSESS. FOR THE KING WHO LACKS UNDERSTANDING IS NO KING AT ALL. BUT MERELY A TYRANT ACTING UPON HIS OWN WHIMS, AND NOT THOSE OF JUSTICE. THIS IS THE REASON WHY SOLOMON, IN ALL OF HIS WISDOM, ASKED GOD FOR A HEART THAT UNDERSTANDS. FOR EVEN IF ONE WERE GIVEN ALL OF THE KNOWLEDGE IN THE WORLD, IT WOULD BENEFIT HIM NOT IF HE DID NOT UNDERSTAND IT. IMAGINE GIVING A CHEST FULL OF PRICELESS JEWELS TO A FOUR-YEAR-OLD CHILD. A MAN BECOMES KING BECAUSE HE HAS A DEEPER THAN NORMAL UNDERSTANDING OF LIFE AND ITS LAWS. THUS, IT FALLS UPON THE SHOULDERS OF THE KING TO PROVIDE UNDERSTANDING TO ALL THOSE IN HIS REALM. ALL GO TO THE KING FOR

UNDERSTANDING, for kings are the light of the **DIVINE** given form here on Earth. Understandings are powerful, for **UNDERSTANDING** is **POWER**. **LOVE** is the highest form of **UNDERSTANDING**. Therefore, a **KING** must understand, for a **KING** must **LOVE**. In fact, a **KING** must be **LOVE** itself.

UNDERSTANDING is the sea from which flows the rivers of **WISDOM**, which settle into lakes of intelligence. If someone were building a wall, the bricks would be **KNOWLEDGE**, the mortar would be **WISDOM**. While the effectiveness of the wall in keeping that which lies behind it safe and sheltered, its sturdiness and longevity would be **UNDERSTANDING**. If someone was cooking pasta, **KNOWLEDGE** would be the ingredients, **WISDOM** would be the recipe, and the taste of the pasta would be **UNDERSTANDING**. One's **UNDERSTANDING** is the manifestation of one's **KNOWLEDGE** and **WISDOM**. A person shapes life and becomes who they are through the

UNDERSTANDINGS THAT THEY POSSESS. IF A MAN POSSESSES ROYAL UNDERSTANDINGS, HE SHALL HAVE A KING'S **UNDERSTANDING** OF LIFE. THUS, A **KING** IS WHAT HE SHALL BE.

THUS, IT IS THAT I SHARE WITH YOU SOME OF MY OWN UNDERSTANDINGS, SO THAT THEY MAY BECOME YOURS AS WELL. I GIVE THESE PROVERBS TO YOU, MY FELLOW KINGS, SO THAT YOU MAY RECEIVE INSTRUCTION AND KNOW **WISDOM.** WHILE THESE ARE NOT ALL OF THE UNDERSTANDINGS THAT A **KING** MUST HAVE, THESE ARE ALL UNDERSTANDINGS THAT A **KING** SHOULD HAVE.

1

A **KING** MUST UNDERSTAND **THE TRUTH**,

UNMISTAKABLE ONCE DISCERNED, IS QUITE OFTEN CONCEALED IN PLAIN SIGHT.

2

A **KING** MUST UNDERSTAND **THE TRUTH** SHALL

ALWAYS BE THE FIRST VICTIM IN A WAR OF OPINIONS.

3

A KING MUST UNDERSTAND ALTHOUGH THE
POTENTIALITY FOR KINGSHIP IS ROOTED WITHIN EVERY MAN'S
SOUL, IT SHALL OFTEN FAIL TO DEVELOP UNLESS IT IS AIDED
BY EDUCATION.

4

A KING MUST UNDERSTAND HE WHO FILLS HIMSELF WITH
THE LIGHT OF **THE TRUTH** SHALL DISSIPATE ALL
DARKNESS WITH HIS PRESENCE.

5

A KING MUST UNDERSTAND ALL FRUSTRATION IS ROOTED
IN IMPATIENCE.

6

A KING MUST UNDERSTAND IT IS WHEN A **KING** CAN
DO WHATEVER HE WANTS THAT THERE IS GREAT DANGER
THAT HE SHALL NOT DO WHAT HE SHOULD.

7

A KING MUST UNDERSTAND IT IS A WEAK DESPICABLE

KING WHO CONTINUALLY GIVES HIS PEOPLE MORE CAUSE FOR DISCORD THAN FOR HARMONY.

8

A KING MUST UNDERSTAND HE WHO HAS MATURED TO THE POINT WHERE HE DESIRES NOTHING MORE THAN TO BE GOOD SHALL NEVER HAVE ANY TROUBLE LEARNING ALL THAT IS NECESSARY.

9

A KING MUST UNDERSTAND THE MOST IMPORTANT INGREDIENTS IN THE RECIPE OF A BEAUTIFUL CONVERSATION ARE HUMILITY AND A THOROUGH KNOWLEDGE OF THE SUBJECT ON WHICH YOU ARE SPEAKING.

10

A KING MUST UNDERSTAND TO BE ENVIED IS TO BE TAXED FOR THE GREATNESS THAT YOU POSSESS.

11

A KING MUST UNDERSTAND A KING WAS MADE TO ACT, NOT BE ACTED UPON.

12

A KING MUST UNDERSTAND YOUR DOMINATION IS COMPLETE WHEN YOU ARE ABLE TO CONVINCE THE OTHER PARTY THAT THEY ARE IN CONTROL.

13

A KING MUST UNDERSTAND GREAT KINGS ARE THOSE REASONABLE AND INTELLIGENT SOULS WITH THE WILL NECESSARY TO DEFINE THEMSELVES AND THEIR OWN CAPABILITIES.

14

A KING MUST UNDERSTAND IT DOES THE ANTELOPE NO GOOD TO PREACH THE GOODNESS OF EATING GRASS TO THE LION.

15

A KING MUST UNDERSTAND ALL GREAT KINGS HAVE AN INNATE ABILITY TO KNOW WHAT THE FUTURE SHALL DEMAND FROM THEM.

16

A KING MUST UNDERSTAND ALL GREAT KINGS BENEFITTED

FROM THE PRACTICE OF HARD WORK.

17

A KING MUST UNDERSTAND BLAME IS A CLEVER TACTIC

THAT THE WEAK USES IN ORDER TO COVER THEIR OWN FAULT

AND SHAME.

18

A KING MUST UNDERSTAND THE LOVE THAT EMANATES

FROM THE PEACE THAT IS SUMMONED IN TIMES OF TURMOIL

MANIFESTS ITSELF AS THE WISDOM THAT SHALL SUBDUE

ALL UNRIGHTEOUSNESS.

19

A KING MUST UNDERSTAND BLESSED IS THE SOUL WHO

HAS THE COURAGE TO ENTER INTO THE PLACE OF DARKNESS,

AND THE STRENGTH TO EMERGE FROM THE SHADOWS

WITH NEW LIGHT.

20

A KING MUST UNDERSTAND ALL THAT COMES EVENTUALLY

LEAVES.

21

A KING MUST UNDERSTAND TO SEE DIFFICULTY AS

OPPORTUNITY IS TO RID YOURSELF OF DIFFICULTIES.

22

A KING MUST UNDERSTAND MOST EXCELLENT IS IT FOR A

KING TO PLEASE THE WOMAN HE LOVES WITHOUT

OFFENDING HER.

23

A KING MUST UNDERSTAND ALL THINGS ARE

INTERTWINED, AND AS A RESULT OF THIS INTERTWINEMENT,

A NATURAL INCLINATION KNOWN AS LOVE IS ALWAYS

PRESENT.

24

A KING MUST UNDERSTAND THE WEAK SHALL FEAR

CHANGE EVEN WHEN THAT CHANGE IS FOR THE BETTER.

25

A KING MUST UNDERSTAND THE DESIRES THAT DOMINATE
YOUR THOUGHTS SHALL MANIFEST AS YOUR REALITY IN TIME.

26

A KING MUST UNDERSTAND AN UGLY MIND HAS NEVER
MANIFESTED A BEAUTIFUL LIFE.

27

A KING MUST UNDERSTAND THE UNIVERSE'S GREATNESS
LIES MANIFEST IN ITS ABILITY TO CONCEAL THE TRUTH.
A KING'S GREATNESS LIES MANIFEST IN HIS ABILITY TO
DISCERN IT.

28

A KING MUST UNDERSTAND THE TRUTH IS THE
ONLY TEACHER IN THE UNIVERSITY OF LIFE, AND THE ONLY
SUBJECT THAT IT TEACHES IS ITSELF.

29

A KING MUST UNDERSTAND ALMIGHTY HUMILITY
DESTROYS ALL SEDITIOUS ENEMIES WITHIN AND HANDS OVER

TO **WISDOM** THE SCEPTER OF ABSOLUTE **POWER**.

30

A KING MUST UNDERSTAND **WISDOM** AND **UNDERSTANDING** SHALL ONLY ARISE IN A MAN WHEN THAT MAN MAKES THE SINCERE DETERMINATION TO SEEK **THE TRUTH**.

31

A KING MUST UNDERSTAND THE ARROGANT ARE SO BECAUSE THEY ARE AFRAID.

32

A KING MUST UNDERSTAND PAIN IS A FRUIT WHICH OFTEN RIPENS UNEXPECTED WITHIN THE FLOWER OF THE PLEASURE THAT CONCEALED IT.

33

A KING MUST UNDERSTAND YOU SHALL NEVER BE ESTEEMED AND RESPECTED MORE HIGHLY THAN WHEN EVERYONE SEES THAT YOU ARE THE CAPTAIN OF YOUR OWN SHIP.

34

A KING MUST UNDERSTAND ONE SHOULD HARDLY EVER CHOOSE TO PRAISE ANYTHING OTHER THAN GREAT MEN AND BRILLIANT DEEDS.

35

A KING MUST UNDERSTAND THE GREATEST HONOR THAT YOU COULD BESTOW UPON ANOTHER IS TO CONCENTRATE YOUR ATTENTION UPON THAT PERSON'S INTEREST.

36

A KING MUST UNDERSTAND HE WHO CONSTANTLY REACTS TO THE ACTIONS OF OTHERS, ALLOWS OTHERS TO CONTROL HIS KINGDOM.

37

A KING MUST UNDERSTAND ONE SHOULD NEVER SEEK COUNSEL FROM AN UNPRODUCTIVE PERSON.

38

A KING MUST UNDERSTAND THE STRENGTH OF A

KING RESIDES IN HIS ABILITY TO **LOVE** GENUINELY.

39

A KING MUST UNDERSTAND RELEASING THINGS OFTENTIMES IS AN ACT OF FAR GREATER **STRENGTH** THAN HOLDING ON TO THEM.

40

A KING MUST UNDERSTAND THE LION WOULD QUICKLY STARVE TO DEATH IF HE MADE IT A HABIT OF TELLING THE ZEBRA WHEN HE WAS APPROACHING.

41

A KING MUST UNDERSTAND BETRAYAL IS THE GREATEST INJURY OF ALL.

42

A KING MUST UNDERSTAND IT IS NOT THE NUMBER OF PEOPLE IN YOUR KINGDOM, BUT THEIR WORTH THAT SHALL MAKE YOUR KINGDOM GREAT.

43

A KING MUST UNDERSTAND THE UNKNOWN HAS BEEN THE COMPANION OF EVERY GREAT VENTURE.

44

A KING MUST UNDERSTAND THE MIGHTIER YOUR ENEMIES ARE, THE GREATER YOUR HONOR IF YOU CONQUER THEM.

45

A KING MUST UNDERSTAND THE ONLY WAY YOUR FORTUNE MAY JUSTLY BE CALLED EVIL IS IF YOU DO NOT FIND A WAY TO MAKE IT BENEFIT YOU.

46

A KING MUST UNDERSTAND ACCEPTING SUFFERING FOR THE BENEFIT OF OTHERS IS THE ESSENCE OF DEVOTION.

47

A KING MUST UNDERSTAND TO ALWAYS MAKE THE BEST OUT OF THE WAY THAT THINGS TURN OUT IS TO ENSURE THAT THINGS ALWAYS TURN OUT FOR THE BEST.

48

A KING MUST UNDERSTAND HE WHO REVEALS THAT HE IS AFRAID THAT HIS LADY MAY LEAVE HIM FOR ANOTHER, BETRAYS HIS FEELINGS OF INFERIORITY TO HIS RIVAL.

49

A KING MUST UNDERSTAND THOSE THAT ONE HATES REFLECTS ONE'S DEEPEST FEARS OF WHAT LIES WITHIN ONESELF.

50

A KING MUST UNDERSTAND DOUBT IS A TRAITOR THAT ALWAYS GIVES FALSE COUNSEL.

51

A KING MUST UNDERSTAND ONLY THAT WHICH YOU BELIEVE POSSIBLE SHALL BE.

52

A KING MUST UNDERSTAND INTELLIGENCE SHALL ALWAYS DEFEAT MIGHT AND STEEL.

53

A KING MUST UNDERSTAND TO NEVER MISTAKE YOUR KNOWLEDGE FOR THE TRUTH IS TO REMAIN EVER OPEN TO THE RECEPTION OF THE TRUTH.

54

A KING MUST UNDERSTAND YOU CAN ONLY FILL YOUR SOUL WITH TRUTH WHEN YOU EMPTY IT OF OPINIONS.

55

A KING MUST UNDERSTAND MAGNANIMITY INFUSES THE SOUL WITH SUCH A POWERFUL INFLUENCE THAT IT TURNS IT TO HONEST WAYS AND ADORNS IT WITH SUCH AN UNSHAKABLE TRANQUILITY THAT IN ALL CIRCUMSTANCES IT REMAINS READY TO RESPOND TO WISDOM AND FOLLOW HER WITH THE UTMOST DOCILITY, LIKE A YOUNG DUCKLING THAT WALKS ALONGSIDE ITS MOTHER, STOPS WHEN SHE DOES, AND MOVES ONLY IN RESPONSE TO HER.

56

A KING MUST UNDERSTAND WISDOM IS A GIFT DESIRED ONLY BY THE WISE.

57

A KING MUST UNDERSTAND ONE SHALL NEVER RECEIVE THAT WHICH THEY REFUSE TO GIVE.

58

A KING MUST UNDERSTAND EVERY EVIL TO WHICH YOU DO NOT SUCCUMB BENEFITS YOU.

59

A KING MUST UNDERSTAND IN ORDER TO BE A GREAT KING, YOU MUST FREE YOURSELF FROM TRADITION, AND LEARN HOW TO MAKE USE OF IT, OR NOT, ACCORDING TO NECESSITY.

60

A KING MUST UNDERSTAND THERE ARE TIMES WHEN EVEN A KING MUST TAKE COMMANDS.

61

A KING MUST UNDERSTAND ONE MUST NEVER ARGUE OVER UNIMPORTANT DETAILS. FOR EVEN IF YOU WIN, YOU SHALL HAVE ONLY WASTED TIME AND MADE YOURSELF PETTY

62

A KING MUST UNDERSTAND A KING CAN NEVER AFFORD TO BE CAUGHT OFF GUARD.

63

A KING MUST UNDERSTAND ONE SHOULD NEVER TELL ANYONE INFORMATION THAT THEY DO NOT WANT TO BE USED AGAINST THEM.

64

A KING MUST UNDERSTAND THE FIRST STEP IN ATTAINING TRUE POWER IS COMING TO THE REALIZATION THAT YOU ARE POWER ITSELF.

65

A KING MUST UNDERSTAND RAGE AND DESPAIR GIVE EVIDENCE TO WEAKNESS, FOR THEY BOTH ENTAIL BEING INJURED, AS WELL AS SUCCUMBING TO ONE'S INJURIES.

66

A KING MUST UNDERSTAND IT IS RIGHT FOR THE CROWN

TO BE HEAVY, BUT WRONG TO ALLOW IT TO CRUSH YOU.

67

A KING MUST UNDERSTAND EDUCATION IS THE KEY THAT

SHALL OPEN THE GATES OF HIGHER CIVILIZATION.

68

A KING MUST UNDERSTAND WORDS ARE INTERPRETATIONS

OF THE TRUTH, AND THUS CAN NEVER BE THE

TRUTH THEMSELVES.

69

A KING MUST UNDERSTAND YOUR LIFE WAS DESIGNED BY

THE DIVINE SO THAT YOU MAY GET EXACTLY WHAT YOU

NEEDED IN ORDER TO DELIVER YOUR OWN EXPRESSION OF

KINGSHIP TO THE WORLD.

70

A KING MUST UNDERSTAND THE MOST BEAUTIFUL

DIAMONDS ARE BORN FROM THE MOST INTENSE PRESSURE.

71

A KING MUST UNDERSTAND A CRISIS IS AN OPPORTUNITY
FOR DEVELOPMENT IN THE PROCESS OF YOUR EVOLUTION.

72

A KING MUST UNDERSTAND WHEN ADVERSITY STRIKES,
ALLOW YOUR MIND TO BE UNMOVED LIKE THE SKY THROUGH
WHICH LIGHTNING TEARS.

73

A KING MUST UNDERSTAND NO MATTER HOW DARK IT
MAY GET, THE STARS SHALL ALWAYS SHINE.

74

A KING MUST UNDERSTAND MEN OFTEN DO THE MOST
FOOLISH THINGS WHEN THEY ARE HEAD OVER HEELS IN
LOVE WITH A WOMAN.

75

A KING MUST UNDERSTAND LOVE IS THE MOTIVATING
FORCE OF LIFE.

76

A KING MUST UNDERSTAND THE HABIT OF DESPAIR IS A HABIT WHICH NO KING CAN AFFORD TO HAVE.

77

A KING MUST UNDERSTAND THAT WHICH YOU THINK, YOU SHALL SAY AND DO. THAT WHICH YOU SAY AND DO SHALL AFFECT YOUR ENTIRE KINGDOM.

78

A KING MUST UNDERSTAND ONE'S BELIEFS SHAPE ONE'S BEHAVIOR, AND ONE'S BEHAVIOR SHALL DETERMINE ONE'S DESTINY.

79

A KING MUST UNDERSTAND TO GO TOO FAR IN A MATTER IS JUST AS BAD AS FALLING SHORT.

80

A KING MUST UNDERSTAND GOODWILL IS ALWAYS WORTH SOMETHING, EVEN FROM THE HUMBLEST OF MEN.

81

A KING MUST UNDERSTAND FROM THE MIND THAT CONSTANTLY HARBORS COMPLAINTS, AND THE FACE THAT HABITUALLY WEARS A FROWN, BEAUTY SHALL FADE, AND IN THE END, VANISH BEYOND HOPE OF EVER BEING RESTORED.

82

A KING MUST UNDERSTAND ONE MOVES FORWARD IN LIFE BY ASKING INTELLIGENT QUESTIONS.

83

A KING MUST UNDERSTAND THE HABIT OF POSSESSING CONTEMPT FOR A THING WITHOUT EXAMINATION IS THE HABIT OF A FOOL.

84

A KING MUST UNDERSTAND HE WHO IS TROUBLED BY DOUBT CANNOT FOCUS UPON SUCCESS. THEREFORE, SEEK NOT TO DEFEAT YOUR ENEMY, BUT RATHER TO DESTROY HIS CONFIDENCE.

85

A KING MUST UNDERSTAND THE BEST WAY TO RECEIVE

FAVOR IS TO DESERVE IT.

86

A KING MUST UNDERSTAND PROBLEMS LIE NOT IN ONE'S

EXPERIENCE, BUT IN ONE'S OPINION OF THEIR EXPERIENCES.

87

A KING MUST UNDERSTAND HE WHO IS HIGHLY

RESPECTED SHALL NOT EASILY BE CONSPIRED AGAINST.

HOWEVER, HE WHO IS HATED AND UNRESPECTED OUGHT TO

FEAR EVERYTHING AND EVERYONE.

88

A KING MUST UNDERSTAND WHATSOEVER MAY OCCUR,

OCCURS BY **DIVINE** DECREE BECAUSE IT IS IN SOME WAY

CONDUCIVE TO YOUR PARTICULAR DESTINY.

89

A KING MUST UNDERSTAND EACH SIDE IN EVERY WAR

BELIEVES THAT THEIR SIDE IS GOOD. THEREFORE, EVERY WAR

EVER FOUGHT IN THE NAME OF GOOD HAS DEPENDED UPON

A LIE.

90

A KING MUST UNDERSTAND ONLY A NOBLE MIND HAS THE STRENGTH TO ACCEPT ITS FATE WITHOUT RESERVATION

OR COMPLAINT.

91

A KING MUST UNDERSTAND IF YOU SEEK VENGEANCE YOU

SHALL RUN INTO RUIN. FOR IT IS PRIDE, AND PRIDE ALONE,

THAT PROMPTS YOU TO IT.

92

A KING MUST UNDERSTAND SELF-CONFIDENCE AND

MENTAL STRENGTH ARE ONE AND THE SAME.

93

A KING MUST UNDERSTAND WHILE YOU MAY BE ABLE TO

PURCHASE A PERSON'S HAND, YOU SHALL NEVER BE ABLE TO

PURCHASE THEIR HEART.

94

A KING MUST UNDERSTAND TO ATTAIN WISDOM, ONE

MUST LEARN TO SEE LIFE AND EVERY SINGLE EVENT WHICH

OCCURS IN IT, AS A TEACHER.

95

A KING MUST UNDERSTAND IT IS ONLY ONCE YOU REALIZE

THAT YOU ARE THE SOURCE OF ALL LOVE THAT YOUR

SEARCH FOR LOVE SHALL END.

96

A KING MUST UNDERSTAND THE VIRTUE OF MAGNANIMITY

IS ESPECIALLY APPROPRIATE FOR A KING. FOR IT GIVES RISE

TO MANY OTHER VIRTUES.

97

A KING MUST UNDERSTAND FEAR IS NAUGHT BUT

ANTICIPATED PAIN.

98

A KING MUST UNDERSTAND EVERYTHING IS LIFE.

HOWEVER, DIFFERENT NAMES ARE GIVEN TO THE MANY

DIFFERENT FORMS THAT IT TAKES. TO DEVELOP THE ABILITY TO SEE BEYOND NAMES AND FORMS IS TO GAIN THE ABILITY TO PERCEIVE **THE TRUTH**.

99

A KING MUST UNDERSTAND IT IS YOUR CURRENT THOUGHTS THAT ARE CURRENTLY CONSTRUCTING YOUR FUTURE KINGDOM.

100

A KING MUST UNDERSTAND THE MAJORITY OF THE **KNOWLEDGE**, FACTS, AND BELIEFS THAT MOST PEOPLE HOLD AS TRUTH ARE INDEED LIES. IT IS THE WISE ONLY THAT ARE ABLE TO CONSISTENTLY DISCERN THE DIFFERENCE BETWEEN TRUTH AND UNTRUTH, YET THE IGNORANT ARE ARROGANT IN THEIR BELIEF THAT THEY ALWAYS CAN, AND ARE THUS THE EASIEST TO FOOL.

101

A KING MUST UNDERSTAND IT IS A DANGEROUS UNDERTAKING TO ATTEMPT TO BE REASONABLE WITH FOOLS.

102

A KING MUST UNDERSTAND IT IS ESSENTIAL THAT A KING FREES HIS WILL FROM THE TYRANNY OF BOTH HIS AND OTHERS' EMOTIONS.

103

A KING MUST UNDERSTAND WHEN THE STUDENT IS READY, LIFE SHALL SUPPLY THE LESSON.

104

A KING MUST UNDERSTAND IT IS ONLY BY PATIENCE, PRACTICE, AND CEASELESS SOLICITATION THAT YOU SHALL BE ALLOWED TO ENTER INTO THE KINGDOM OF KNOWLEDGE, WISDOM, AND UNDERSTANDING.

105

A KING MUST UNDERSTAND EMOTIONAL PEOPLE ARE VULNERABLE PEOPLE OVER WHOM ONE CAN EASILY EXERT POWER.

106

A KING MUST UNDERSTAND WHILE MANY RECEIVE ADVICE,

ONLY THE WISE PROFIT FROM IT.

107

A KING MUST UNDERSTAND IT SHALL ALWAYS BE BETTER

TO DO GOOD TODAY THAN TO BECOME GOOD ON ANOTHER.

108

A KING MUST UNDERSTAND THE KING WHO REFUSES

TO BE GREAT DOES A GREAT WRONG TO HIS KINGDOM.

109

A KING MUST UNDERSTAND ONE MUST ALWAYS ENDEAVOR

TO BEND AND SWAY WITH THE WINDS OF TIME, RATHER

THAN STAND FIXED AND IMMOBILE AGAINST THEM. FOR

NOTHING ABOUT LIFE IS STATIC AND UNCHANGING.

110

A KING MUST UNDERSTAND MANY ARE THE TRIALS AND

TRIBULATIONS OF THE GREAT.

111

A KING MUST UNDERSTAND IN THINGS DISHONORABLE, YOU ARE NOT OBLIGATED TO OBEY ANYONE.

112

A KING MUST UNDERSTAND FAILURE LIES ONLY IN ONE'S REFUSAL TO GET BACK UP.

113

A KING MUST UNDERSTAND IT IS A PART OF EVERY GREAT KING'S GREATNESS THAT THEY PROFIT FROM EVERY EXPERIENCE.

114

A KING MUST UNDERSTAND AFTER THE STRUGGLE YOU SHALL HAVE NO DOUBT DEFEATED THE DEMON.

115

A KING MUST UNDERSTAND HE WHO WRONGS ANOTHER DOES INJUSTICE TO HIMSELF BY MAKING HIMSELF BAD.

116

A KING MUST UNDERSTAND TO REFUSE TO VIEW
WHATEVER HAPPENS AS EVIL, IS TO PREVENT HARM FROM EVER
COMING UPON YOU.

117

A KING MUST UNDERSTAND BECAUSE ALL MEN ARE BORN,
LIVE, AND DIE, EACH ACCORDING TO THE SAME RULES, ONE
MUST NEVER DOUBT THAT THEY CAN DO WHATEVER ANY
OTHER HAS DONE BEFORE THEM.

118

A KING MUST UNDERSTAND CONFIDENCE IS WHEN YOU
ASK YOURSELF FOR THE ANSWER AND EXPECT IT TO BE RIGHT.

119

A KING MUST UNDERSTAND TO LOVE, YOU MUST SERVE,
SACRIFICE FOR, LISTEN TO, EMPATHIZE WITH, APPRECIATE,
AND AFFIRM THOSE THAT YOU WISH TO LOVE.

120

A KING MUST UNDERSTAND PATIENCE WORKS SILENTLY

LIKE A SECRET PROTECTOR THAT SHALL PREVENT YOU FROM
GETTING CAUGHT UP IN THE TRAPS OF POINTLESS ACTION
AND DESPAIR.

121

A KING MUST UNDERSTAND IT IS IMPOSSIBLE TO HAVE A
RELATIONSHIP WITH SOMEONE THAT YOU REFUSE TO PAY
ATTENTION TO.

122

A KING MUST UNDERSTAND TO BE JUST, TEMPERATE,
STRONG, WISE, MUNIFICENT, AND CLEMENT IS TO GAIN THE
FAVOR OF THE **DIVINE**, THROUGH WHOSE GRACE YOU
SHALL ACQUIRE THAT HEROIC VIRTUE, WHICH SHALL RAISE
YOU ABOVE HUMAN LIMITATIONS, AND MAKE YOU CAPABLE OF
BEING REGARDED AS MORE THAN A MORTAL MAN.

123

A KING MUST UNDERSTAND THE **DIVINE** REJOICES IN
AND PROTECTS THOSE KINGS THAT STRIVE TO RESEMBLE IT IN
GOODNESS AND **WISDOM**.

124

A KING **MUST UNDERSTAND** TO DISCOVER YOUR COURAGE ALL YOU MUST DO IS LEARN TO IGNORE YOUR FEARS.

125

A KING **MUST UNDERSTAND** WRONG IDEAS CAN WARP THE JUDGMENT OF EVEN THE MOST REASONABLE, AND MANY ARE THEY THAT HAVE BEEN MISLED BY OPINIONS.

126

A KING **MUST UNDERSTAND** ALL THAT YOU ARE IS ALL THAT YOU HAVE THOUGHT.

127

A KING **MUST UNDERSTAND** TO FEAR THAT SOMETHING MAY BE, IS THE FIRST STEP IN DRAWING IT INTO YOUR REALITY.

128

A KING **MUST UNDERSTAND** JUST BECAUSE A BIRD IS BORN IN AN OVEN DOESN'T MAKE IT A LOAF OF BREAD. FOR NO MATTER WHERE A BIRD IS BORN, ITS DESTINY IS TO GROW UP

AND FLY AMONGST THE CLOUDS.

129

A KING MUST UNDERSTAND YOUR KINGDOM IS A
REFLECTION OF YOUR THOUGHTS.

130

A KING MUST UNDERSTAND SOMETIMES THE ORDINARY IS
EXTRAORDINARY SIMPLY BECAUSE IT IS UNEXPECTED.

131

A KING MUST UNDERSTAND A MAN'S WILL TO DO IS BORN
FROM THE BELIEF THAT HE IS ABLE TO DO.

132

A KING MUST UNDERSTAND THE MASSES SHALL ALWAYS
GIVE RESPECT AND ATTENTION TO THE EXTRAORDINARY.

133

A KING MUST UNDERSTAND EVEN IF YOU ARE ON THE
ROAD TO GREATNESS, YOU SHALL GET RUN OVER IF YOU
CHOOSE TO SIMPLY SIT THERE.

134

A KING MUST UNDERSTAND A KING SHOULD ALWAYS BE MODEST IN VICTORY AND GRACEFUL IN DEFEAT.

135

A KING MUST UNDERSTAND IF YOUR BROTHER FALLS, NEVER BOAST YOURSELF ABOVE HIM. FOR YOU KNOW NOT IF YOU WOULD HAVE BEEN ABLE TO WITHSTAND THAT SAME TEMPTATION.

136

A KING MUST UNDERSTAND ONE SHOULD NEVER CONFINE THEIR EXPRESSION OF ESTEEM TO THE RICH AND POWERFUL ALONE. FOR THOSE WHO ARE POOR AND WEAK TODAY MAY BE RICH AND POWERFUL TOMORROW.

137

A KING MUST UNDERSTAND IN ADVERSITY, ACTION REVEALS SECRETS WHICH DEJECTION AND DESPONDENCY WOULD HAVE CONCEALED FOREVER.

138

A KING MUST UNDERSTAND UNDER ALL CIRCUMSTANCES,
A KING MUST REMAIN DIGNIFIED AND RESPECTABLE.

139

A KING MUST UNDERSTAND ACHIEVEMENT IS THE RESULT
OF ONE'S STRUGGLE AGAINST OPPOSITION.

140

A KING MUST UNDERSTAND THE UNLEASHING OF ANGER
WITHOUT FORETHOUGHT IS A MOST DANGEROUS
INDULGENCE, AND THE USE OF THREATS IS THE MOST
FOOLISH KIND OF EXPOSURE.

141

A KING MUST UNDERSTAND THE SUN IS ALWAYS SHINING,
WHETHER IT IS COVERED BY THE CLOUDS OR NOT.

142

A KING MUST UNDERSTAND IT IS IMPOSSIBLE TO LIVE IN A
WORLD WHERE LIARS, VILLAINS, OR SHAMELESS PEOPLE DID
NOT EXIST. AND TO WISH FOR THE IMPOSSIBLE IS

SOMETHING A **KING** MUST NOT DO.

143

A KING MUST UNDERSTAND NOTHING SHALL EVER HAPPEN
TO YOU WHICH LIFE DOES NOT APPROVE.

144

A KING MUST UNDERSTAND SUFFERING IS THE FIRE IN
WHICH IGNORANCE BURNS ITSELF UP.

145

A KING MUST UNDERSTAND THE PERSON WHO MAKES A
WRONG CHOICE IS STILL IN A BETTER POSITION THAN HE
WHO IS TOO AFRAID TO MAKE A CHOICE AT ALL.

146

A KING MUST UNDERSTAND A GRATEFUL DOG IS WORTH
MORE THAN AN UNGRATEFUL MAN.

147

A KING MUST UNDERSTAND THERE IS NO WOMAN THAT
CAN RESIST THE PULL OF A SECRET DESIRE THAT HAS COME TO

148

A KING MUST UNDERSTAND NO KING EVER HAD A POINT OF PRIDE THAT DID NOT INJURE HIM.

149

A KING MUST UNDERSTAND ALL THE WORLD LOVES A LOVER.

150

A KING MUST UNDERSTAND INTELLECTUAL VIRTUE IS PERFECTED BY STUDY, AND MORAL VIRTUE IS PERFECTED BY PRACTICE.

151

A KING MUST UNDERSTAND A KING POSSESSES THAT RARE COURAGE ONLY FOUND IN CERTAIN MEN, WHICH ALWAYS FORCES ONE TO MOVE FORWARD.

152

A KING MUST UNDERSTAND ALL FOOLS CONFUSE THEIR

153

A KING MUST UNDERSTAND THE HARVEST REAPED

DEPENDS SOLELY UPON THE SEEDS PLANTED.

154

A KING MUST UNDERSTAND HE WHO REFUSES TO ACCEPT

THE TRUTH IS DESTINED TO BE ASSASSINATED BY LIES.

155

A KING MUST UNDERSTAND ON THE PATH OF LIFE, IT IS

JOY THAT PROPELS ONE FORWARD.

156

A KING MUST UNDERSTAND THERE EXISTS NOT A HELL

WHERE THE DEVIL DOES NOT RULE.

157

A KING MUST UNDERSTAND A TEACHER CAN ONLY

EFFECTIVELY TEACH THOSE THAT HE UNDERSTANDS.

158

A KING MUST UNDERSTAND MANY GIVE IN TO VANITY WHEN SUCCESS IS ASSURED AND RAPIDLY FALL BACK INTO FAILURE.

159

A KING MUST UNDERSTAND EVEN MORE IMPORTANT THAN THE CONTENT OF YOUR MESSAGE IS ITS FORM. FOR EVEN THE BEST MESSAGES ARE USELESS IF NO ONE DESIRES TO LISTEN TO THEM.

160

A KING MUST UNDERSTAND GRATITUDE IS THE FORCE THAT SHALL ATTRACT ALL GOOD THINGS INTO YOUR KINGDOM.

161

A KING MUST UNDERSTAND IT IS NOT YOUR RESPONSIBILITY TO DO WHAT YOU LACK THE POWER TO DO.

162

A KING MUST UNDERSTAND RAGE AND LAMENTATIONS HARM YOU MORE THAN THAT WHICH WAS THEIR CAUSE.

163

A KING MUST UNDERSTAND NO MATTER HOW POWERFUL YOU BECOME, YOU MUST ALWAYS REMEMBER THAT THERE IS SOMETHING BEHIND THE THRONE THAT IS GREATER THAN THE CROWN.

164

A KING MUST UNDERSTAND A GOOD TEACHER SHALL ALWAYS BE A GOOD STUDENT.

165

A KING MUST UNDERSTAND ALL FLIGHTS HAVE BEGUN WITH A FALL.

166

A KING MUST UNDERSTAND ADVERSITIES ARE PERFECT OPPORTUNITIES TO DISPLAY YOUR KINGLY POISE.

167

A KING MUST UNDERSTAND A MAN'S HABITS AND

MANNERS DETERMINE THE QUALITY OF MAN HE SHALL BE.

168

A KING MUST UNDERSTAND NO MATTER WHAT HAPPENS,

IT IS ALWAYS WRONG FOR A **KING** TO DESPAIR.

169

A KING MUST UNDERSTAND ONE SHOULD NEVER ALLOW

AN OLD GRUDGE TO AFFECT NEW CHOICES.

170

A KING MUST UNDERSTAND NOTHING SHALL EVER HAPPEN

TO YOU WHICH NATURE HAS NOT GIVEN YOU THE **POWER**

TO ENDURE.

171

A KING MUST UNDERSTAND IT IS ESSENTIAL THAT YOU SEE

TO IT THAT YOU ARE NEVER TO BE BLAMED FOR EXPECTING A

LIAR TO TELL **THE TRUTH.**

172

A KING MUST UNDERSTAND YOU SHOULD WISH NOT TO
BE RID OF AN ENEMY, BUT RATHER TO BE RID OF YOUR
DESIRE TO BE RID OF AN ENEMY.

173

A KING MUST UNDERSTAND THERE SHALL COME A TIME IN
THE LIFE OF EVERY KING WHEN HE MUST, WITHOUT
KNOWING WHAT LIES AHEAD, MAKE A CHOICE THAT SHALL
INFLUENCE ALL THE EVENTS IN HIS LIFE TO FOLLOW.

174

A KING MUST UNDERSTAND A VINDICTIVE MAN WOULD
RATHER USE A SLEDGEHAMMER WHEN A FEATHER WOULD DO.

175

A KING MUST UNDERSTAND A SHARED JOURNEY WITH A
BIT OF HARDSHIP SHALL DO MORE TO CREATE A DEEP AND
LASTING BOND WITH A WOMAN THAN SHALL EXPENSIVE
GIFTS.

<h1 style="text-align:center">176</h1>

A KING MUST UNDERSTAND THE HANDS OF THE KING ARE THE HANDS OF A HEALER, AND IT IS THUS THAT THE RIGHTFUL KING SHALL BE MADE KNOWN.

<h1 style="text-align:center">177</h1>

A KING MUST UNDERSTAND THERE IS NOTHING MORE DREADFUL AND SAD THAN THE PAINFUL PANGS OF HOPELESS LOVE.

<h1 style="text-align:center">178</h1>

A KING MUST UNDERSTAND HE WHO LACKS KNOWLEDGE EASILY FALLS INTO VICE.

<h1 style="text-align:center">179</h1>

A KING MUST UNDERSTAND WHEN YOU REMOVE FEAR FROM A SITUATION, ALL THAT REMAINS IS LOVE.

<h1 style="text-align:center">180</h1>

A KING MUST UNDERSTAND THE TRUTH NEEDS NO DEFENSE.

181

A KING MUST UNDERSTAND IF YOU BELIEVE YOU CAN DO A THING, YOUR BELIEF SHALL ALLOW YOU TO DO IT. IF YOU BELIEVE YOU CANNOT DO A THING, YOUR BELIEF SHALL NOT ALLOW YOU TO DO IT.

182

A KING MUST UNDERSTAND HE WHO REFUSES TO LISTEN SHALL NEVER BE ABLE TO COMPREHEND **THE TRUTH**.

183

A KING MUST UNDERSTAND ALTHOUGH AMBITION MAY INVITE YOU TO CLIMB QUICKLY TO EXTREME HEIGHTS, REMEMBER THE WIND IS STRONGER AT THOSE HEIGHTS, THE FOOTING MORE TENTATIVE, AND THE FALL MUCH FARTHER.

184

A KING MUST UNDERSTAND THE NARROWER THE MIND THAT SPEAKS, THE BROADER THE STATEMENTS IT SHALL UTTER.

185

A KING MUST UNDERSTAND TO BECOME IMMUNE TO THE OPINIONS OF OTHERS IS TO CEASE BEING UNDER THE CONTROL OF OTHERS.

186

A KING MUST UNDERSTAND THE STRENGTH OF YOUR EFFORT SHALL BE THE MEASURE OF YOUR RESULT.

187

A KING MUST UNDERSTAND THE FAULT INHERENT IN A FAILURE TO COMMUNICATE DOES NOT RESIDE IN THE AUDIENCE, BUT IN HE WHO IS COMMUNICATING TO THAT AUDIENCE.

188

A KING MUST UNDERSTAND INNER JOY IS THE FUEL OF SUCCESS.

189

A KING MUST UNDERSTAND BEFORE YOU GET ANGRY WITH SOMEONE THAT DECEIVED YOU, OR SOMEONE WHO WAS

UNGRATEFUL TO YOU, FIRST, GET ANGRY WITH YOURSELF FOR

TRUSTING A LIAR, OR DOING GOOD DEEDS WITH STRINGS

ATTACHED.

190

A KING MUST UNDERSTAND A CHILD'S INTELLIGENCE IS

FAR GREATER THAN ITS CAPACITY TO EXPRESS ITSELF.

191

A KING MUST UNDERSTAND WHAT OTHERS THINK AND

DO IS OF THE UTMOST IRRELEVANCE COMPARED TO WHAT

YOU YOURSELF THINK AND DO.

192

A KING MUST UNDERSTAND DESTINY SO ADMIRES

GREATNESS THAT SHE CHOOSES TO REVEAL IT THROUGH

ADVERSITY.

193

A KING MUST UNDERSTAND UNSOCIABLE MANNERS ARE

ALWAYS A MOST DEPLORABLE THING.

194

A KING MUST UNDERSTAND BETRAYAL IS OFTEN A

WOUNDING THAT PROVIDES AN OPENING TO A NEW LIFE.

195

A KING MUST UNDERSTAND ALL GREAT DEEDS REQUIRE

GREAT SACRIFICE.

196

A KING MUST UNDERSTAND JUST AS A PHYSICIAN SHALL

PRESCRIBE UNPLEASANT TREATMENTS IN ORDER TO CURE A

PATIENT OF SICKNESS, SO TOO SHALL LIFE PRESCRIBE

UNPLEASANTNESS IN ORDER TO CURE A MAN OF HIS

WEAKNESS.

197

A KING MUST UNDERSTAND ONLY YOU HAVE THE

POWER TO MANIFEST THAT WHICH YOU DESIRE TO

EXPERIENCE.

198

A KING MUST UNDERSTAND ALL WHO BEHAVE

INCORRECTLY ACT IN THAT MANNER AS A RESULT OF THEIR

IGNORANCE. FOR THERE IS NONE SO VILE THAT THEY DO

NOT RESENT BEING CALLED UNJUST, GREEDY, OR WRONG.

199

A KING MUST UNDERSTAND EVERY PERSON THAT IS ABLE

TO REASON HAS THE **POWER** TO CONVERT EVERY

HINDRANCE INTO MATERIAL THAT THEY CAN USE TO

FURTHER THEIR OWN AMBITIONS.

200

A KING MUST UNDERSTAND ONE CANNOT GO UP

WITHOUT FIRST BEING LOW, AND THERE IS NO **HONOR**

THAT IS NOT PRECEDED BY HUMILITY.

201

A KING MUST UNDERSTAND THE GREATEST OF ALL

MOTIVES IS **LOVE**.

202

A KING MUST UNDERSTAND DILIGENCE IS NAUGHT BUT

CONCENTRATED PATIENCE.

203

A KING MUST UNDERSTAND A KING IS AS FIERCE AND LOYAL IN LOVE AS HE IS IN WAR.

204

A KING MUST UNDERSTAND JUST AS THE AIM OF A DOCTOR SHOULD BE TO GUIDE HIS PATIENTS TO HEALTH, THE AIM OF A KING SHOULD BE TO GUIDE HIS PEOPLE TO VIRTUE.

205

A KING MUST UNDERSTAND TO FEAR SOMETHING IS TO GIVE THAT SOMETHING POWER OVER YOU.

206

A KING MUST UNDERSTAND AS ONE'S YOUTH DECLINES, THEIR WISDOM SHALL INCREASE. FOR NATURE REFUSES TO BESTOW ALL HER GIFTS AT ONE TIME.

207

A KING MUST UNDERSTAND EVERY THOUGHT THAT YOU HAVE SHALL EITHER BRING YOU CLOSER TO LOVE OR PUSH

208

A KING MUST UNDERSTAND EVEN AMONGST A CROWD OF LIES, **THE TRUTH** HAS THE **POWER** TO STAND ALONE.

209

A KING MUST UNDERSTAND THE **KING** WHO WISHES, ABOVE ALL ELSE, TO BE REMEMBERED FONDLY FOR SERVING THE BEST INTEREST OF HIS FOLLOWERS SHALL RULE THE MOST WISELY.

210

A KING MUST UNDERSTAND A BELIEF IS MERELY A THOUGHT THAT ONE HABITUALLY THINKS

211

A KING MUST UNDERSTAND WHAT IS, IS WHAT WAS MEANT TO BE.

212

A KING MUST UNDERSTAND HESITATION IS A POISON

CAPABLE OF KILLING EVEN THE STRONGEST OF DREAMS.

213

A KING MUST UNDERSTAND JUST AS DRIPPING WATER IS ABLE TO WEAR THROUGH STONE, SO TOO CAN THE SUBMISSIVE AND YIELDING SUBDUE THE STUBBORN AND STRONG.

214

A KING MUST UNDERSTAND SOMETIMES THE ORDINARY IS EXALTED TO THE EXTRAORDINARY SIMPLY BECAUSE OF ITS PLACE IN TIME.

215

A KING MUST UNDERSTAND NO MATTER WHAT YOUR CIRCUMSTANCES, OR MATERIALS YOU HAVE TO WORK WITH, THERE IS NOTHING THAT CAN PREVENT YOU FROM DOING THE VERY BEST YOU CAN WITH THEM.

216

A KING MUST UNDERSTAND MANY THAT HAVE WORN A CROWN HAVE BEEN POSSESSED BY PRIDE, AND NOT A FEW

HAVE FALLEN VICTIM TO THEIR OWN SENSE OF SELF-

IMPORTANCE.

217

A KING MUST UNDERSTAND DILIGENCE ALLOWS YOU TO

MANEUVER THE CIRCUMSTANCES OF YOUR LIFE TO YOUR OWN

ADVANTAGE, WHILE PROCRASTINATION ALLOWS

CIRCUMSTANCES TO PUSH YOU INTO FAILURE.

218

A KING MUST UNDERSTAND YOU MUSTN'T CONCERN

YOURSELF WITH THE RAIN. INSTEAD, YOU MUST LEARN TO

WALK BETWEEN THE RAINDROPS.

219

A KING MUST UNDERSTAND ALL WORDS ARE CHILDISH

AND IDLE UNLESS THEY ARE CONCERNED WITH SOME SUBJECT

OF IMPORTANCE.

220

A KING MUST UNDERSTAND WHEN THE DARKNESS

DEPARTS AND THE DAY COMES, THE SUN SHALL SHINE THAT

MUCH BRIGHTER FOR THE MEMORY OF THE DARK.

221

A KING MUST UNDERSTAND AT ALL TIMES, A KING MUST REMAIN BOTH EAGER AND PREPARED TO LEARN.

222

A KING MUST UNDERSTAND WHERE THERE IS LIFE, A GOOD LIFE IS POSSIBLE.

223

A KING MUST UNDERSTAND EVEN THOSE WHO ARE NOT PERFECTLY ENDOWED BY NATURE CAN, THROUGH CARE AND EFFORT, POLISH, AND TO A GREAT EXTENT, CORRECT THEIR NATURAL DEFECTS.

224

A KING MUST UNDERSTAND UGLINESS EXISTS SO THAT BEAUTY MAY BE RECOGNIZED.

225

A KING MUST UNDERSTAND LOVE IS POWERLESS WHERE

226

A KING MUST UNDERSTAND ALTHOUGH THE DIVINE HAS NO FAVORITES, IT ALWAYS SIDES WITH THOSE THAT HAVE A PURE HEART.

227

A KING MUST UNDERSTAND ONE GROWS TO LOVE ONLY THOSE THINGS WHICH THEY KNOW AND UNDERSTAND.

228

A KING MUST UNDERSTAND IT IS ONLY WHEN THE EARS OF A STUDENT ARE READY THAT UNDERSTANDING LIPS SHALL COME FORTH TO FILL THEM WITH WISDOM.

229

A KING MUST UNDERSTAND A WOMAN CAN RESIST ANYTHING BUT ATTENTION.

230

A KING MUST UNDERSTAND IT IS VERY RARE THAT

231

A KING MUST UNDERSTAND THERE IS A TENDENCY TO ECHO THOSE WHOM ONE FEARS AND HATES, SO THAT THEIR POWER MAY BE ATTAINED.

232

A KING MUST UNDERSTAND A KING MUST ALWAYS PLACE HIS HEART IN THE BOSOM OF SERENITY SO THAT SHE MAY GUIDE AND TURN IT WHEREVER SHE SEES FIT.

233

A KING MUST UNDERSTAND THE CHANGES IN YOUR CIRCUMSTANCES SHALL BE IN DIRECT CORRELATION WITH THE CHANGES IN YOUR THOUGHTS.

234

A KING MUST UNDERSTAND ONLY INFORMATION IS GIVEN IN BOOKS. NEVER THE TRUTH.

235

A KING MUST UNDERSTAND A FOOL REJECTS WHAT HE SEES

FOR WHAT HE THINKS.

236

A KING MUST UNDERSTAND YOU SHALL BECOME
WHATEVER IT IS THAT YOUR MIND DWELLS UPON.

237

A KING MUST UNDERSTAND HISTORY IS MERELY A FABLE
THAT THE MASSES HAVE AGREED WITH.

238

A KING MUST UNDERSTAND TO KNOW AND NOT DO IS TO
NOT KNOW.

239

A KING MUST UNDERSTAND TO REACT INSTEAD OF
STRATEGIZE IS A SIGN OF WEAKNESS IN ONE'S CHARACTER.

240

A KING MUST UNDERSTAND THOSE WHO COME TO YOU
FOR AID TODAY MAY VERY WELL BE THE SOURCE OF YOUR
SALVATION TOMORROW.

241

A KING MUST UNDERSTAND DISCRETION SHALL DO
WONDERS TO BEAUTIFY THE SPEECH OF A KING.

242

A KING MUST UNDERSTAND THE COMMON MAN SEEKS TO
BE INSPIRED. A KING IS INSPIRATION ITSELF.

243

A KING MUST UNDERSTAND TO OPEN YOUR MOUTH IS TO
PLACE YOURSELF AT THE MERCY OF ALL THOSE LISTENING.

244

A KING MUST UNDERSTAND CIRCUMSTANCES DO NOT
MAKE A KING. THEY ONLY REVEAL WHO THE KING IS.

245

A KING MUST UNDERSTAND THE WAY A KING BEHAVES
NECESSARILY GOVERNS THE BEHAVIOR OF ALL.

246

A KING MUST UNDERSTAND BEING ATTACKED MEANS

THAT YOU ARE IMPORTANT ENOUGH TO BE A TARGET.

247

A KING MUST UNDERSTAND DIGGING FOR FACTS IS FAR MORE INTELLIGENT THAN JUMPING TO CONCLUSIONS.

248

A KING MUST UNDERSTAND NOTHING HAPPENS OUTSIDE OF THE ONE REALITY OF LIFE. THUS, ALL THAT OCCURS, HAPPENS BY DESIGN.

249

A KING MUST UNDERSTAND LIFE HAS NOT SET SUCH LIMITS ON HUMAN DIGNITIES THAT A MAN MAY NOT ASCEND FROM ONE TO ANOTHER.

250

A KING MUST UNDERSTAND THOSE THAT LOVE EVIL SHALL HAVE IT AS A CONSTANT COMPANION.

251

A KING MUST UNDERSTAND LOVE IS CAPABLE OF

ROBBING ONE OF THEIR FREE WILL USING NO OTHER WEAPON

BESIDES ITSELF.

252

A KING MUST UNDERSTAND A STUBBORN MAN SHALL

ALWAYS BE BURDENED WITH TROUBLES. FOR STUBBORNNESS

BRINGS ONLY MISFORTUNE.

253

A KING MUST UNDERSTAND EVERY GREAT KING HAS

HAD TO LEARN TO MASTER AND DIRECT THE POWER

GENERATED BY THE EMOTION OF LOVE.

254

A KING MUST UNDERSTAND WISDOM IS ALWAYS

FOUND ALONGSIDE PATIENCE.

255

A KING MUST UNDERSTAND EVEN A MAN WITH NO EYES IS

ABLE TO SEE BETTER THAN A MAN WITH NO HEART.

256

A KING MUST UNDERSTAND BEAUTY IS THE SUPREME ADORNMENT OF EVERYTHING. THUS, TO CALL ANYTHING BEAUTIFUL CONSTITUTES THE HIGHEST PRAISE.

257

A KING MUST UNDERSTAND SELF-DOUBT, IF YOU ARE STRONG ENOUGH TO IGNORE IT, SHALL BECOME A POWERFUL ALLY THAT SHALL RAISE YOU TO THE HEIGHTS OF GLORY. HOWEVER, IF YOU INDULGE IT, IT SHALL BECOME AN ENEMY WHICH SHALL CAST YOU DOWN TO THE DEPTHS OF DESPAIR.

258

A KING MUST UNDERSTAND IN ALL OF YOUR ACTIONS, YOU MUST DISPLAY COURAGE, GRAVITY, AND FORTITUDE. FOR THESE ARE THE VIRTUES THAT SHALL CAUSE YOU TO BE HELD IN AWE.

259

A KING MUST UNDERSTAND WHETHER INTELLIGENTLY CULTIVATED OR ALLOWED TO RUN WILD, YOUR MIND SHALL BRING FORTH A CROP.

260

A KING MUST UNDERSTAND A KING MUST, ABOVE ALL ELSE, GUARD HIS SPIRIT FROM THE DESPICABLE VICES OF FICKLENESS, FRIVOLITY, MEAN-SPIRITEDNESS, AND IRRESOLUTENESS. FOR TO DISPLAY THESE CHARACTERISTICS IS TO BE HELD IN CONTEMPT.

261

A KING MUST UNDERSTAND THE MAN WHO LEAVES MUST NEVER LOOK BACK.

262

A KING MUST UNDERSTAND HE WHO PURIFIES HIS MIND GAINS THE ENTIRE WORLD AS A FRIEND.

263

A KING MUST UNDERSTAND TO THOSE WHO ARE IN THE WRONG AND DESERVING OF REPROOF, THERE IS NOTHING MORE PLEASING THAN TO RECEIVE SYMPATHY AND PRAISE.

264

A KING MUST UNDERSTAND SOMETIMES IT IS BETTER TO

BE EXPLOITED THAN MARGINALIZED. FOR IF ONE IS BEING
EXPLOITED IT CAN AT LEAST BE ASSUMED THAT THEY ARE
NEEDED.

265

A KING MUST UNDERSTAND POWER LIES NOT IN WHAT
YOU BELIEVE, BUT IN THE BELIEF ITSELF.

266

A KING MUST UNDERSTAND THE ENERGY YOU EMANATE
SHALL BE THE ENERGY THAT YOU ATTRACT.

267

A KING MUST UNDERSTAND A KING SHOULD EITHER
SPEAK WISELY OR REMAIN SILENT.

268

A KING MUST UNDERSTAND A KING SHOULD NEVER SAY
ANYTHING THAT IS NOT WORTH THE TIME TO SAY.

269

A KING MUST UNDERSTAND IT IS MORE DAMAGING FOR A

KING TO SAY FOOLISH THINGS THAN IT IS FOR HIM TO DO

THEM.

270

A KING MUST UNDERSTAND THE DARKER THE SKY, THE

BRIGHTER THE STARS SHALL SHINE.

271

A KING MUST UNDERSTAND THE RULE OF A KING

SHOULD NOT BE IMPERIOUS LIKE THAT OF A MASTER OVER HIS

SLAVES, BUT SWEET AND CALM, LIKE THAT OF A GOOD FATHER

OVER A GOOD SON.

272

A KING MUST UNDERSTAND ON HIS PATH TO THE

THRONE, A KING MUST LEARN TO MAKE HIS ENEMIES THE

GRAVEL BENEATH HIS FEET AND THE STEPPING STONES TO HIS

GREATNESS.

273

A KING MUST UNDERSTAND IF YOU WOULD BUT SERVE,

YOU SHALL BE SERVED IN RETURN.

274

A KING MUST UNDERSTAND BEYOND EXCESS, EVEN THE
SWEETEST NECTAR CAN BECOME A POISON.

275

A KING MUST UNDERSTAND A KING IS MADE A KING
BY HIS CHOICES AND THE AGREEMENTS THAT HE MAKES WITH
LIFE.

276

A KING MUST UNDERSTAND YOU MUST NEVER ALLOW THE
WRONGS OF ANOTHER TO DISTURB YOU.

277

A KING MUST UNDERSTAND TO LOVE AND RESPECT
YOURSELF IS TO BE LOVED AND RESPECTED.

278

A KING MUST UNDERSTAND WISDOM ADOPTS AND
BECOMES THE MOTHER TO ALL THOSE WHO SEARCH HER OUT.

279

A KING MUST UNDERSTAND HE THAT LOVES, INTEGRATES THE MAGNIFICENCE OF THAT WHICH HE LOVES INTO HIS OWN GREATNESS.

280

A KING MUST UNDERSTAND GENTLENESS SHALL FORCE OTHERS MUCH MORE OFTEN THAN FORCE SHALL MOVE OTHERS TO GENTLENESS.

281

A KING MUST UNDERSTAND A WOMAN SHALL NEVER SHOW A BOY HOW MUCH SHE TRULY KNOWS ABOUT MEN.

282

A KING MUST UNDERSTAND AS YOU GROW IN CHARACTER, STRENGTH, WISDOM, AND HUMILITY, YOUR KINGDOM SHALL GROW IN PROPORTION.

283

A KING MUST UNDERSTAND HOPE IS THE ONE FRIEND THAT SHALL NEVER FORSAKE YOU.

284

A KING MUST UNDERSTAND BRAVERY IS ALWAYS
RESPECTED. EVEN BY AN ENEMY.

285

A KING MUST UNDERSTAND YOU ALONE ARE THE MASTER
GARDENER OF YOUR MIND.

286

A KING MUST UNDERSTAND THE TRUTH DOES NOT
NEED A VERSE ATTACHED TO IT TO BE TRUE.

287

A KING MUST UNDERSTAND EACH POSITION IN EVERY
CONFLICT HAS ITS OWN TRUTH AS FELT BY EACH SIDE.

288

A KING MUST UNDERSTAND A KING IS ONLY GOOD
WHEN HIS PEOPLE ARE SEEN TO BE GOOD.

289

A KING MUST UNDERSTAND JUST AS ONLY THOSE WHO

OPEN A CURTAIN SHALL RECEIVE LIGHT INTO A ROOM, ONLY

THOSE WHO OPEN THEIR MINDS SHALL RECEIVE WISDOM

INTO THEIR SOULS.

290

A KING MUST UNDERSTAND TIME IS A RIVER THAT CARRIES

EVERYTHING AWAY IN ITS CURRENT AT THE VERY MOMENT

THAT IT IS SEEN.

291

A KING MUST UNDERSTAND THE REAL BEGINNINGS OF

YOUR INFLUENCE SHALL COME AS OTHERS SENSE THAT YOU

ARE BEING INFLUENCED BY THEM.

292

A KING MUST UNDERSTAND TO STOP A PERSON FROM

DOING SOMETHING, YOU MUST FIRST FIND A WAY TO MAKE

THEM STOP WANTING TO DO IT.

293

A KING MUST UNDERSTAND THERE ARE MANY MEN WHO

ARE NOTHING MORE THAN THE TITLES ACCORDED TO THEM

294

A KING MUST UNDERSTAND WHEREVER A RIGHTEOUS MAN SPEAKETH, THERE IS **POWER**.

295

A KING MUST UNDERSTAND WHATEVER YOU ARE, SO ALSO SHALL THE MEN BELOW YOU BE.

296

A KING MUST UNDERSTAND A GREAT **KING** MUST ALWAYS BE WILLING TO BE LITTLE.

297

A KING MUST UNDERSTAND THE BEST BLADES ARE THOSE THAT HAVE BEEN FORGED IN THE HOTTEST FIRES.

298

A KING MUST UNDERSTAND GOOD HABITS ARE STRENGTHENERS OF THE SOUL.

299

A KING MUST UNDERSTAND THOSE WHO ARE NOT WITH YOU DURING YOUR ADVERSITY SHALL NOT BE WITH YOU DURING YOUR PROSPERITY. EVEN IF THEY DARE NOT SHOW THIS OPENLY.

300

A KING MUST UNDERSTAND NO ONE EVER APPROVES OF HE WHO BEGS FOR APPROVAL.

301

A KING MUST UNDERSTAND FAILURES ARE MERELY STEPPING STONES TO ACHIEVEMENT.

302

A KING MUST UNDERSTAND THE WISE KING CHOOSES TO FOCUS MORE UPON HIS FUTURE THAN HIS PAST, AND HIS PRESENT MORE THAN BOTH.

303

A KING MUST UNDERSTAND ONLY THE IGNORANT BELIEVE THAT THERE IS SOMETHING EVIL ABOUT BEING EITHER POOR

304

A KING MUST UNDERSTAND THE MORE A HEART IS WORTH CAPTURING, THE MORE DIFFICULT IT SHALL BE TO WIN.

305

A KING MUST UNDERSTAND IF YOU LEARN TO VALUE KNOWLEDGE AND WISDOM IN YOUR YOUTH, THEY SHALL NOT FORSAKE YOU WHEN YOU GROW OLD.

306

A KING MUST UNDERSTAND THERE CAN BE NO TRUE LOVE WHERE THERE IS NO SACRIFICE.

307

A KING MUST UNDERSTAND IT IS POSSIBLE TO KNOW A GREAT DEAL AND YET UNDERSTAND VERY LITTLE.

308

A KING MUST UNDERSTAND THERE IS NO ENDEAVOR IN ALL THE WORLD MORE WORTHWHILE THAN MAKING A

309

A KING MUST UNDERSTAND A NOBLE HEART SHALL ALWAYS

BE FOUND IN THE MAN WHO PERSEVERES.

310

A KING MUST UNDERSTAND IT IS ONLY BY IDENTIFYING

AND FACING YOUR FEARS THAT YOU SHALL BE ABLE TO TAKE

AWAY THEIR COVERT POWER TO DETERMINE YOUR LIFE.

311

A KING MUST UNDERSTAND THE GREATER YOUR

COURTESY, THE GREATER SHALL BE YOUR RENOWN, YOUR

FAME, AND YOUR GLORY.

312

A KING MUST UNDERSTAND ALL THOUGHTS BEAR FRUIT

AFTER THEIR OWN KIND.

313

A KING MUST UNDERSTAND AMONGST THE MASSES, THE TRUTH IS OFTEN DROWNED IN A SEA OF OPINIONS.

314

A KING MUST UNDERSTAND THE SECRET TO THE STRENGTH OF A KING LIES IN HIS ABILITY TO REMAIN CALM AND DETACHED IN TIMES OF PERIL.

315

A KING MUST UNDERSTAND WHATEVER YOU WISH TO SEE OUTSIDE MUST FIRST HAPPEN WITHIN YOU.

316

A KING MUST UNDERSTAND ALL PHENOMENA PERCEIVED ARE BUT DROPLETS OF WATER FLOWING IN THE RIVER OF TIME.

317

A KING MUST UNDERSTAND MONEY IS THE DAZZLER OF MANY AND IS CAPABLE OF PERVERTING EVEN THE CHARACTER OF THE KINGS.

318

A KING MUST UNDERSTAND THE SOURCE OF A KINGDOM'S STRENGTH IS ITS UNITY.

319

A KING MUST UNDERSTAND THE ART OF KINGSHIP IS THE MOST DISTINGUISHED AND RAREST OF ALL THE ARTS.

320

A KING MUST UNDERSTAND A MAGNANIMOUS KING HAS SUCH AN AIR OF GREATNESS ABOUT HIM, ACCOMPANIED BY SUCH A GRACIOUS HUMILITY THAT THE WORLD ITSELF SHALL ALWAYS SEEM TOO LIMITED FOR HIM.

321

A KING MUST UNDERSTAND THE BEST WAY TO MOTIVATE PEOPLE IS NOT THROUGH REASON BUT EMOTION.

322

A KING MUST UNDERSTAND HE WHO IS WILLING TO DIE IN ORDER TO ACCOMPLISH HIS GOALS SHALL ALWAYS HAVE THE ADVANTAGE OVER HE THAT IS NOT.

323

A KING MUST UNDERSTAND IT IS ONLY THROUGH SUFFERING THAT YOU SHALL FIND THE TRUE MEASURE OF YOUR **STRENGTH**.

324

A KING MUST UNDERSTAND IT IS THE DUTY OF A GOOD KING TO KNOW THE CHARACTER AND INCLINATIONS OF HIS PEOPLE.

325

A KING MUST UNDERSTAND THERE LIES NO GOOD IN WAITING UNTIL DANGER IS UPON YOU TO PREPARE YOURSELF FOR IT.

326

A KING MUST UNDERSTAND JUST AS TREES BEND LOW WITH RIPENED FRUIT AND CLOUDS HANG LOW WITH RAIN, SO TOO DOES A NOBLE **KING** BOW GRACIOUSLY. FOR THIS IS THE WAY OF GENEROUS THINGS.

327

A KING MUST UNDERSTAND SUFFERING IS PAIN THAT ONE CHOOSES TO HOLD ON TO.

328

A KING MUST UNDERSTAND INDECISION IS A MURDERER THAT SLAYS MILLIONS OF ASPIRATIONS DAILY.

329

A KING MUST UNDERSTAND WHEREVER LIFE MAY TAKE YOU, YOU MUST ALWAYS BEAR IN MIND YOUR DUTY TO BE GREAT.

330

A KING MUST UNDERSTAND LOVE CAN ONLY BE ATTRACTED BY LOVE.

331

A KING MUST UNDERSTAND WHEN A WOMAN CRITICIZES YOU, SHE DOES SO IN ORDER TO FORCE YOU INTO A SUPERIOR POSITION SO THAT SHE MAY BE ABLE TO THRUST THE ROLE OF HERO UPON YOU.

332

A KING MUST UNDERSTAND WHILE SUCCESS BEGINS WITH

HUMILITY, FAILURE BEGINS WITH STUBBORN ARROGANCE.

333

A KING MUST UNDERSTAND ONLY HE THAT IS VALUED, ESTEEMED, AND LOVED SHALL BE MISSED IN HIS ABSENCE

334

A KING MUST UNDERSTAND ULTIMATE WISDOM SHALL NOT MANIFEST ITSELF IN A SPIRIT WHOSE EQUILIBRIUM CAN BE DISTURBED BY THE EVIL WHICH EXISTS IN THE WORLD.

335

A KING MUST UNDERSTAND LOVE VANQUISHES ALL ATTACKS, AND IS IMPREGNABLE IN DEFENSE.

336

A KING MUST UNDERSTAND HUMILITY IS ESSENTIAL TO THE OUTCOME OF WHETHER OR NOT A MAN SHALL MAKE A GREAT KING.

337

A KING MUST UNDERSTAND IT IS ONLY ONCE YOU FREE

338

A KING MUST UNDERSTAND A WISE KING RULES BY
INTELLIGENCE, CHARISMA, RESPECT, AND THE ABILITY TO
COMBINE ALL OF HIS PEOPLE'S DIVERGENT INTERESTS INTO
ONE GENERAL INTEREST BY WHICH THEY ARE ALL BENEFITTED.

339

A KING MUST UNDERSTAND IT IS THE WISE KING THAT
DIRECTS HIS ENERGIES WITH INTELLIGENCE AND
FORETHOUGHT, AND ORIENTATES HIS THOUGHTS TO
FRUITFUL ISSUES.

340

A KING MUST UNDERSTAND TRUTH CAN NEVER BE
ESTABLISHED BY CONSENSUS. IF SOMETHING IS TRUE, IT
DOESN'T MATTER HOW MANY PEOPLE BELIEVE IT.

341

A KING MUST UNDERSTAND THERE IS NO WORSE

CATASTROPHE THAT CAN BEFALL A **KING** THAN TO BE
REDUCED TO SUCH STRAITS THAT HE CAN NEITHER ACCEPT
THE CONDITIONS OF PEACE, NOR SUPPORT THE DIFFICULTIES
OF WAR.

342

A KING MUST UNDERSTAND HE WHO IS KEEN TO LEARN
REJECTS NOTHING.

343

A KING MUST UNDERSTAND ON THE STAGE OF LIFE, ALL
OF THE DRAMAS THAT HAVE PLAYED OUT IN PREVIOUS TIMES
ARE OCCURRING NOW, AND SHALL REOCCUR IN THE FUTURE.
ONLY WITH DIFFERENT ACTORS.

344

A KING MUST UNDERSTAND THE OPPRESSED OFTEN RISE
TO THE THRONE, AND SOME THAT NONE WOULD CONSIDER
SHALL ONE DAY WEAR A CROWN.

345

A KING MUST UNDERSTAND THE GREATEST AND MOST

ESSENTIAL STEP THAT YOU MUST TAKE IN ORDER FOR YOU TO ASCEND TO THE THRONE IS FOR YOU TO TAKE RESPONSIBILITY FOR THE CREATION OF YOUR KINGDOM.

346

A KING MUST UNDERSTAND MASTERY IS THE RESULT OF REPETITION AND PRACTICE. FOR IT IS PRACTICE THAT MAKES THE MASTER.

347

A KING MUST UNDERSTAND BECAUSE YOU ARE UNIQUE IN THE ENTIRE HISTORY OF CREATION, YOU YOURSELF HAVE A UNIQUE GIFT TO OFFER IT.

348

A KING MUST UNDERSTAND GREAT KINGS ARE ALWAYS VALIANT AND MANNERLY. IN THEIR DEALINGS WITH EACH OTHER, IN SERVING THEIR LADIES, AND IN ALL OF THEIR ACTIONS, THEY BEHAVE WITH THE UTMOST COURTESY AND DISCRETION.

349

A KING MUST UNDERSTAND A GREAT KING IS SO BLESSED THAT SIMPLY BY KNOWING HIM, OTHERS' LIVES AUTOMATICALLY BECOME BETTER.

350

A KING MUST UNDERSTAND A KING ACTS AS A KING BECAUSE HE IS A KING, AND A KING IS A KING BECAUSE HE ACTS AS A KING.

351

A KING MUST UNDERSTAND IT IS FAR EASIER TO AVOID A QUARREL THAN IT IS TO EMERGE VICTORIOUS FROM ONE.

352

A KING MUST UNDERSTAND TESTING PERIODS OF ADVERSITY ARE A GREAT PRIVILEGE TO YOU WHEN THEY COME. FOR THESE ARE THE TESTS THAT SHALL GIVE YOU AN OPPORTUNITY TO TAKE INVENTORY OF YOUR INNER SELF.

353

A KING MUST UNDERSTAND A KING'S GREATNESS SHOULD

ALWAYS BE ACCOMPANIED BY A CERTAIN FRIENDLY GENTLENESS, A GRACIOUS AND AMIABLE HUMANITY, AND AN ACCOMPLISHED MANNER OF DISCREETLY FAVORING BOTH YOUR PEOPLE AND STRANGERS IN VARYING DEGREES, EACH ACCORDING TO THEIR MERIT.

354

A KING MUST UNDERSTAND THE BLOW THAT KNOCKS YOU OFF YOUR FEET IS NOT SO MUCH THE HARD BLOW AS THE ONE THAT YOU DO NOT SEE COMING.

355

A KING MUST UNDERSTAND IT IS IMPOSSIBLE TO HURT OR HELP ANOTHER WITHOUT DOING THE SAME TO YOURSELF.

356

A KING MUST UNDERSTAND THE NOBLEST WAY TO TAKE REVENGE ON ANOTHER IS TO REFUSE TO BE LIKE THEM.

357

A KING MUST UNDERSTAND A DECISIVE MAN CANNOT BE STOPPED FROM REACHING HIS GOAL, BUT AN INDECISIVE MAN

CANNOT GET STARTED PURSUING HIS DREAMS.

358

A KING MUST UNDERSTAND IGNORANCE IN ITS BLINDNESS IS INCAPABLE OF SEEING THE SUFFERING THAT IT INFLICTS UPON BOTH ITSELF AND OTHERS.

359

A KING MUST UNDERSTAND WOMAN IS INDEED YOUR GREATEST DANGER. FOR SHE SHALL DEMAND FROM YOU YOUR GREATEST.

360

A KING MUST UNDERSTAND THE POOR MAN WHO IS WISE SHALL SOON BE THOUGHT OF AS SOMEONE GREAT.

361

A KING MUST UNDERSTAND A BIRD SHALL ALWAYS SING MORE PRETTILY IF YOU ARE ABLE TO CONVINCE IT TO WALK INTO A CAGE ON ITS OWN.

362

A KING MUST UNDERSTAND HUMILITY AND COMPASSION

ARE THE MAIN SYMPTOMS OF THE CONDITION OF

WISDOM.

363

A KING MUST UNDERSTAND WINE AND WOMEN CAN MAKE

SENSIBLE MEN DO FOOLISH THINGS.

364

A KING MUST UNDERSTAND THE GLORIOUS VIRTUE OF

STRENGTH CAN ONLY BE DEVELOPED THROUGH

PRACTICE AND EFFORT.

365

A KING MUST UNDERSTAND HOPE IS THE LIGHT THAT

SIGNALS THE END OF THE DARK NIGHT OF DESPAIR.

366

A KING MUST UNDERSTAND THERE IS GREAT HONOR

TO BE FOUND IN LOYALTY.

367

A KING MUST UNDERSTAND HE WHO HAS STRENGTHENED AND PURIFIED HIS THOUGHTS HAS NO NEED TO FEAR OR EVEN CONSIDER THE MALEVOLENT.

368

A KING MUST UNDERSTAND **THE TRUTH** IS LIKE A GREAT MOUNTAIN. SOLID AND IMMOVABLE, WHETHER YOU LIKE, OR EVEN CHOOSE TO ACKNOWLEDGE IT.

369

A KING MUST UNDERSTAND IT IS THE NATURE OF BASE SPIRITS TO BE INSOLENT IN PROSPERITY, AND POOR AND ABJECT IN ADVERSITY.

370

A KING MUST UNDERSTAND THE MINDS OF MEN SHALL ALWAYS DETEST THOSE THINGS WHICH HAVE ACCOMPANIED THEIR SORROWS, AND **LOVE** THOSE THINGS WHICH HAVE ACCOMPANIED THEIR JOYS.

371

A KING MUST UNDERSTAND A PUZZLE FITS TOGETHER ONLY BECAUSE ALL OF ITS PIECES ARE DIFFERENT.

372

A KING MUST UNDERSTAND PEOPLE ARE ALWAYS VULNERABLE TO INSINUATIONS THAT STROKE THEIR VANITY.

373

A KING MUST UNDERSTAND THE POWER YOUR WORDS SHALL HAVE OVER YOUR PEOPLE DEPEND UPON YOUR PEOPLE'S BELIEF IN THEM.

374

A KING MUST UNDERSTAND EVERY MAN IS A WORSE MAN WHEN HE ACTS WITH THE MASSES RATHER THAN ACTING ALONE.

375

A KING MUST UNDERSTAND A GREAT KING CREEPS LIKE A MOUSE, BUT HAS THE JAWS OF A LION.

376

A KING MUST UNDERSTAND ONLY A FOOL WOULD SHOW

HIS CARDS WHEN THE GAME HAS JUST BEGUN.

377

A KING MUST UNDERSTAND THERE IS NOTHING MORE

IMPORTANT TO PEOPLE'S VANITY THAN THEIR INTELLIGENCE.

378

A KING MUST UNDERSTAND THERE IS NO SUCH THING AS

DEFEAT OR FAILURE UNLESS YOU ACCEPT THEM AS SUCH.

379

A KING MUST UNDERSTAND IF YOU ARE RIGHTEOUS, YOUR

PEOPLE SHALL REJOICE.

380

A KING MUST UNDERSTAND IT IS THE WISE THAT NOTES

THE INDICATIONS OF DANGERS, AND THUS AVOIDS THEM.

381

A KING MUST UNDERSTAND A GREAT KING MAKES

EVERYONE WITH WHOM THEY INTERACT FEEL THE INNER

GLOW WHICH COMES FROM BEING APPRECIATED.

382

A KING MUST UNDERSTAND IT IS MOST DISGRACEFUL

WHEN A MAN'S SPIRIT FAILS BEFORE HIS BODY DOES.

383

A KING MUST UNDERSTAND YOU, AND ONLY YOU, ARE

RESPONSIBLE FOR ALL THE GOOD AND BAD IN YOUR LIFE.

384

A KING MUST UNDERSTAND WHILE FOOLISHNESS IS

RELATIVELY HARMLESS, AN INTELLIGENT FOOL IS EXTREMELY

DANGEROUS.

385

A KING MUST UNDERSTAND THERE SHOULD BE NOTHING

SURPRISING TO YOU ABOUT A FOOL ACTING FOOLISH.

386

A KING MUST UNDERSTAND IN LOVE, THE WOMAN

387

A KING MUST UNDERSTAND EVERY GREAT PERSON

RECOGNIZES **WISDOM** AND SHALL BESTOW **HONOR**

UPON ALL THOSE THAT SHOW IT.

388

A KING MUST UNDERSTAND THE MOST FORTUNATE PEOPLE

IN THIS WORLD ARE THOSE WHO HAVE BEEN LOVED SINCE

THEIR BIRTH.

389

A KING MUST UNDERSTAND IT IS A BRAVE MAN THAT

ACKNOWLEDGES THE STRENGTHS OF OTHERS.

390

A KING MUST UNDERSTAND REASONABLE WOMEN WERE

MADE FOR REASONABLE MEN.

391

A KING MUST UNDERSTAND IT IS THE STRONG, CALM MAN

WHO IS ALWAYS LOVED AND REVERED.

392

A KING MUST UNDERSTAND ANGER MAKES EVEN A

TRUSTED FRIEND AN ENEMY.

393

A KING MUST UNDERSTAND IF ALL OF YOUR

INTERACTIONS WITH OTHERS ARE PERFORMED WITH LOVE,

RESPECT, AND CONSIDERATION, LIFE ITSELF SHALL ENFOLD

YOU IN THE PROTECTIVE LIGHT OF JUSTICE.

394

A KING MUST UNDERSTAND VILE THOUGHTS ARE THE

SHACKLES OF FATE.

395

A KING MUST UNDERSTAND ACHIEVEMENT IS THE CROWN

OF EFFORT.

396

A KING MUST UNDERSTAND THERE IS NO RELIGION HIGHER THAN THE TRUTH.

397

A KING MUST UNDERSTAND THE HIGHER YOU LIFT YOUR THOUGHTS, THE GREATER SHALL BE YOUR SUCCESS, AND THE MORE BLESSED AND ENDURING SHALL BE YOUR ACHIEVEMENTS.

398

A KING MUST UNDERSTAND SOME AVOID THE TRUTH WHEN IT IS PAINFUL. YOU SHALL ONLY BECOME KING WHEN YOU DEVELOP THE DISCIPLINE TO OVERCOME THAT PAIN.

399

A KING MUST UNDERSTAND WHATSOEVER IS ACQUIRED UNJUSTLY IS RARELY PRESERVED.

400

A KING MUST UNDERSTAND ANXIETY AND FEAR ARE THE

MARKS OF SPIRITUAL IMMATURITY. FOR HE WHO GROWS
ANXIOUS AND FEARFUL LACK **FAITH** IN HIMSELF.

401

A **KING** MUST UNDERSTAND EVERYTHING THAT YOU NOW
SEE SHALL BE SOON FORGOTTEN AND SWALLOWED BY THE
ABYSS OF ETERNITY.

402

A **KING** MUST UNDERSTAND IF YOU TALK TO A MAN
ABOUT HIMSELF HE SHALL LISTEN FOR HOURS.

403

A **KING** MUST UNDERSTAND HE WHO IS UNABLE TO
ACCEPT AUTHORITY HIMSELF IS UNABLE TO RULE HIMSELF,
AND THUS UNFIT TO SIT ON THE THRONE.

404

A **KING** MUST UNDERSTAND TREES GROW NOT ONLY
UPWARD, BUT DOWNWARD AS WELL. THEREFORE, NO
KING SHOULD EVER DISOWN HIS DARK ROOTS.

405

A KING MUST UNDERSTAND A KING IS A FORCE OF

NATURE THAT BRINGS HARMONY AND COHERENCE.

406

A KING MUST UNDERSTAND THERE IS NOTHING TO BE

GAINED BY LAMENTING WHAT NEVER WAS.

407

A KING MUST UNDERSTAND INTENSITY SHALL ALWAYS

DEFEAT EXTENSITY.

408

A KING MUST UNDERSTAND SELF-RELIANCE IS THE WEAPON

WHICH SHALL DEFEAT ALL ADVERSITIES.

409

A KING MUST UNDERSTAND YOU MUST FIRST SEEK THE

CHARACTER OF A KING BEFORE YOU SEEK THE TITLE OF A

KING.

410

A KING MUST UNDERSTAND NO KING HAS EVER

BECOME GREAT WITHOUT HAVING A GREAT ENEMY.

411

A KING MUST UNDERSTAND THE CONSTANT FLOW OF LIFE

SHALL AGAIN AND AGAIN DEMAND FROM YOU FRESH

ADAPTATION. FOR ADAPTATION IS NEVER ACHIEVED ONCE

AND FOR ALL.

412

A KING MUST UNDERSTAND ONCE YOU WAKE UP, YOU

SHALL SEE THAT IT WAS ONLY DREAMS THAT TROUBLED YOU.

413

A KING MUST UNDERSTAND ALTHOUGH THERE IS ONLY

ONE LIFE, ALL ARE FREE TO SHAPE IT THROUGH THE CHOICES

THAT THEY MAKE.

414

A KING MUST UNDERSTAND THERE SHALL NEVER BE A

SITUATION BETTER SITUATED FOR THE PRACTICE OF

GOODNESS THAN THE ONE IN WHICH YOU NOW FIND

YOURSELF.

415

A KING MUST UNDERSTAND IT IS EXTREMELY DIFFICULT

FOR ONE TO REFUSE ANYTHING TO ONE BY WHOM THEY FEEL

THEY ARE DEARLY LOVED.

416

A KING MUST UNDERSTAND A SECRET IN THE MOUTH OF

A FOOL IS LIKE A SPLINTER IN THE FINGER.

417

A KING MUST UNDERSTAND IT IS ONLY POSSIBLE TO

ATTRACT AND HOLD ON TO AS MUCH LOVE AS YOU FEEL

FOR YOURSELF.

418

A KING MUST UNDERSTAND HUBRIS IS A FATAL

COMPANION. FOR IT MAKES A FOOL OUT OF EVEN THE

GREATEST OF MEN.

419

A KING MUST UNDERSTAND A KING IS LOVE, AND LOVE MAKES EVERYTHING GROW.

420

A KING MUST UNDERSTAND THE MORE TRANQUIL YOU BECOME, THE GREATER SHALL BE YOUR SUCCESS, INFLUENCE, AND POWER FOR GOOD.

421

A KING MUST UNDERSTAND DEATH IN ITSELF IS NOTHING, FOR EVERYONE DIES. BUT TO LIVE DEFEATED, TO SIMPLY GIVE UP, IS TO DIE EVERY DAY THAT YOU LIVE.

422

A KING MUST UNDERSTAND IT IS YOUR ABILITY TO SEE BEAUTY IN ALL CIRCUMSTANCES THAT SHALL GIVE YOUR LIFE MEANING.

423

A KING MUST UNDERSTAND ANY IDEA CAN BE IMPLANTED WITHIN SOMEONE'S MIND, SIMPLY BY BEING REPEATED OFTEN

424

A KING MUST UNDERSTAND REALITY HAS TWO SIDES. ON ONE SIDE, YOU HAVE THE OBJECT OF PERCEPTION. THIS IS THE TRUTH. ON THE OTHER SIDE, YOU HAVE ONE'S POINT OF VIEW, WHICH IS MERELY ONE'S INTERPRETATION OF THE TRUTH.

425

A KING MUST UNDERSTAND MEN, ALL HAVING THE SAME ORIGIN, ARE EQUALLY ANCIENT, AND NATURE HAS MADE NO DIFFERENCE IN THEIR POTENTIAL TO BE.

426

A KING MUST UNDERSTAND ALL NEGATIVE EMOTIONS HAVE THEIR FOUNDATIONS IN FEAR.

427

A KING MUST UNDERSTAND ALL THINGS FADE AWAY, BECOMING EITHER THE STUFF OF LEGEND, OR BURIED IN OBLIVION.

428

A KING MUST UNDERSTAND THE ONE THING PEOPLE SHALL NEVER GROW TIRED OF IS HAVING THEIR OWN SELF-WORTH VALIDATED.

429

A KING MUST UNDERSTAND IT IS A LOT HARDER TO STOP A RIVER THAN IT IS TO REDIRECT IT TO A USEFUL PURPOSE.

430

A KING MUST UNDERSTAND THE GREATEST OF FOOLS ARE OFTENTIMES WISER THAN THOSE THAT LAUGH AT THEM.

431

A KING MUST UNDERSTAND IN ORDER TO BE SEEN AS A KING, IT IS NECESSARY THAT YOU HAVE THE PRESENCE OF A KING.

432

A KING MUST UNDERSTAND THERE IS NO EXCUSE FOR BEING UNPREPARED.

433

A KING MUST UNDERSTAND YOU SHALL NEVER BE UNDONE BY THE MISTAKES YOU MAKE. ONLY BY HOW YOU RESPOND TO THEM.

434

A KING MUST UNDERSTAND FAILURE AND PAIN ARE THE LANGUAGES WHICH NATURE SPEAKS TO ALL CREATURES THAT SHE WISHES TO ACQUIRE UNDERSTANDING.

435

A KING MUST UNDERSTAND YOU MUST NEVER DISCOUNT EVEN THE SLIGHTEST WORD THAT SOMEONE UTTERS AS FRIVOLOUS. FOR GREAT THINGS ARE OFTEN FOUND IN SMALL TALK.

436

A KING MUST UNDERSTAND SHORT-TERM DEFEAT IS FAR BETTER THAN LONG-TERM DISASTER.

437

A KING MUST UNDERSTAND AS KING, YOU HAVE BEEN

SINGLED OUT BY A **DIVINE** CHOICE THAT WAS MADE AT
THE BEGINNING OF TIME.

438

A KING MUST UNDERSTAND ALL KINGS HAVE A
SIGNIFICANT PART TO PLAY IN THE **DIVINE** DRAMA
KNOWN AS THE HISTORY OF THE WORLD.

439

A KING MUST UNDERSTAND IT IS IMPERATIVE THAT YOU
RISE ABOVE THE TRANSITORINESS OF ORDINARY HUMAN
EXISTENCE, SO THAT YOU MAY REACH A NEW AND HIGHER
STATE OF **DIGNITY** AND IMPORTANCE.

440

A KING MUST UNDERSTAND EVERY EVENT WHICH OCCURS
IN YOUR LIFE IS EITHER FOR YOUR BENEFIT, OR BRINGS UP
WHAT YOU NEED TO LOOK AT IN ORDER TO CREATE GOOD
FOR YOURSELF.

441

A KING MUST UNDERSTAND THE WIND CAN NEVER FAVOR

YOUR SAILS IF YOU REFUSE TO CHOOSE A DIRECTION.

442

A KING MUST UNDERSTAND JUST AS WISE SPEECH IS NOT A CHARACTERISTIC OF ONE WHO POSSESSES A FOOLISH HEART, LYING LIPS ARE NOT A CHARACTERISTIC OF ONE WHO POSSESSES THE HEART OF A KING.

443

A KING MUST UNDERSTAND DILIGENCE IS GREATLY AIDED BY FEELINGS OF AFFECTION AND AN ANXIETY TO PLEASE.

444

A KING MUST UNDERSTAND IF YOU LEARN TO APPRECIATE WISDOM WHEREVER YOU HEAR IT, YOU SHALL SOON BECOME WISE AND YOUR WORDS, IN TURN, SHALL BECOME A SOURCE OF WISDOM FOR OTHERS.

445

A KING MUST UNDERSTAND LOVE ALWAYS DESIRES TO GROW. YOU NEED ONLY TO PLANT THE SEEDS.

446

A KING MUST UNDERSTAND THERE IS ALWAYS SOMETHING BEAUTIFUL TO BE FOUND. YOU ONLY NEED TO LOOK FOR IT.

447

A KING MUST UNDERSTAND LOVE IS THE RECOGNITION OF ONENESS IN THIS WORLD OF DUALITY. THUS, TO LOVE ANOTHER IS TO RECOGNIZE YOURSELF IN ANOTHER.

448

A KING MUST UNDERSTAND THE GREATER YOU ARE, THE MORE YOU MUST HUMBLE YOURSELF.

449

A KING MUST UNDERSTAND DOUBT IS THE MOST TREACHEROUS ENEMY OF A KING.

450

A KING MUST UNDERSTAND KINDNESS GIVEN IS KINDNESS RECEIVED. ALWAYS BE KIND TO OTHERS. FOR THE BASIC TENET OF GETTING ALONG, BEING HAPPY, AND ENLISTING THE ASSISTANCE OF OTHERS TOWARDS ACHIEVING ALL THAT

YOU DESIRE IS THAT PEOPLE WANT TO HELP AND DO THINGS
FOR YOU.

451

A KING MUST UNDERSTAND YOU SHALL BRING TO A
NATURAL AND LOGICAL CONCLUSION WHATEVER THOUGHTS
YOU PERMIT TO DOMINATE YOUR MIND.

452

A KING MUST UNDERSTAND A PERSON'S BELIEF SYSTEM
DOESN'T SHOW THEM WHAT IS TRUE. IT ONLY SHOWS THEM
WHAT THEY BELIEVE.

453

A KING MUST UNDERSTAND IN A LAND WHERE THERE IS
FEAR OF FAMINE, FEAR OF DEATH, AND PRISONS THAT ARE
OVERWHELMINGLY FULL, THERE IS NO ROOM LEFT IN THE
MINDS OF THE PEOPLE FOR APPREHENSIONS OF EVIL OR HELL.

454

A KING MUST UNDERSTAND WHAT THE IGNORANT CALL
LOVE IS OFTEN MERELY A POSSESSIVENESS AND ADDICTIVE

CLINGING THAT IS ABLE TO TURN INTO HATE IN AN INSTANT.

455

A KING MUST UNDERSTAND EVEN THE GREATEST OF CITIES

WERE AND ARE BUT MERE HOUSEHOLDS IN THE GREAT CITY

THAT IS THE WORLD.

456

A KING MUST UNDERSTAND IN SOCIETY EVERYONE WEARS

A MASK AND PRETENDS TO BE MORE SURE OF THEMSELVES

THAN THEY IN FACT ARE.

457

A KING MUST UNDERSTAND HE THAT DEFINES, RULES.

458

A KING MUST UNDERSTAND TO KNOW WHAT A MAN

WANTS IS TO KNOW WHO HE IS AND HOW TO MOVE HIM.

459

A KING MUST UNDERSTAND A KING IS AN OPENING

THROUGH WHICH THE LOVE OF THE UNIVERSE FLOWS

FROM THE UNMANIFEST SOURCE OF ALL LIFE FOR THE BENEFIT

OF THE WORLD.

460

A KING MUST UNDERSTAND YOU MUST NEVER BETRAY
YOURSELF FOR FAME. FOR FAME IS MERELY THE FUTURE
GOSSIP OF OTHERS.

461

A KING MUST UNDERSTAND THE BOLD ARE ADMIRED BY
ALL. THE TIMID BY NONE.

462

A KING MUST UNDERSTAND DEFEAT IS NOTHING MORE
THAN AN INSPIRATION FOR A GREATER AND MORE PERSISTENT
EFFORT.

463

A KING MUST UNDERSTAND THE FIRST STEP IN LEARNING
HOW TO RULE IS LEARNING HOW TO RULE YOURSELF.

464

A KING MUST UNDERSTAND THE ONLY REAL ENDING IN

THIS LIFE IS DEATH. EVERYTHING ELSE IS MERELY A
TRANSITION.

465

A KING MUST UNDERSTAND HE THAT REPEATEDLY HAS
THE NEED TO TELL OTHERS THAT HE IS **KING** IS NO TRUE
KING AT ALL.

466

A KING MUST UNDERSTAND IT IS NOT ONLY IN YOUR
POWER NOT TO BE UPSET WITH THE RUDE AND
UNGRATEFUL, BUT EVEN TO SHOW THEM COMPASSION.

467

A KING MUST UNDERSTAND THE DECISIONS OF YOUR
PRESENT ARE THE ARCHITECTS OF YOUR FUTURE.

468

A KING MUST UNDERSTAND FOR NEITHER **LOVE** NOR
GAIN MUST YOU EVER FIGHT ON THE SIDE IN ANY QUARREL
THAT IS NOT RIGHTEOUS.

469

A KING MUST UNDERSTAND IT IS A MUCH GREATER FAULT TO BE FOUND LACKING IN LOVE THAN LACKING IN PRUDENCE.

470

A KING MUST UNDERSTAND IGNORANCE IS A QUALITY WHICH YOU MUST NEVER BOAST OF HAVING.

471

A KING MUST UNDERSTAND IT IS BY FEELING THE ACHE OF LONELINESS THAT THE HEART OPENS UP TO RECEIVE MORE LOVE.

472

A KING MUST UNDERSTAND SELF-DOUBT AND HUMILITY ARE NOT THE SAME THING.

473

A KING MUST UNDERSTAND AN HOUR SPENT IN HATRED IS AN ETERNITY WITHDRAWN FROM LOVE.

474

A KING MUST UNDERSTAND A POOR MAN'S WISDOM

LIFTS HIS HEAD HIGH AND SETS HIM AMONGST KINGS.

475

A KING MUST UNDERSTAND THE REAL GREATNESS OF A

MAN IS MEASURED BY THE POWER OF THE FEELINGS THAT

HE CONTROLS. NOT THOSE THAT CONTROL HIM.

476

A KING MUST UNDERSTAND EVEN IF YOU ARE OTHERWISE

PERFECT, YOU SHALL FAIL IF YOU LACK HUMILITY.

477

A KING MUST UNDERSTAND THE ONLY LIMITATIONS THAT

YOU HAVE ARE THE ONES WHICH YOU CREATE IN YOUR OWN

MIND.

478

A KING MUST UNDERSTAND IT SHALL ALWAYS BE BETTER

TO ASK A QUESTION AND GET THE TRUTH THAN TO

MAKE AN ASSUMPTION AND GET A LIE.

479

A KING MUST UNDERSTAND IT IS AN UNDERTAKING OF THE UTMOST DANGER TO ENTERPRISE THE LIBERTY OF A PEOPLE THAT ARE RESOLVED TO BE SLAVES.

480

A KING MUST UNDERSTAND EVERY TRUE KING HAS A MISSION TO FULFILL RATHER THAN A MERE POSITION TO OCCUPY.

481

A KING MUST UNDERSTAND YOU ARE A CELL IN THE BODY OF THE SINGLE ORGANISM OF ALL INTELLIGENT LIFE KNOWN AS THE UNIVERSE.

482

A KING MUST UNDERSTAND PEOPLE ARE PRONE TO TRUST ANYTHING OVER WHICH THEY BELIEVE THEY HAVE CONTROL.

483

A KING MUST UNDERSTAND WHILE MANY MISTAKE STRONG PASSIONS FOR A STRONG CHARACTER, HE WHO IS

MASTERED BY HIS PASSIONS IS A WEAK MIND.

484

A KING MUST UNDERSTAND IT IS THE WEAKNESS OF EVERY
FOOL, THAT HE LOVES TO HEAR THAT HE IS IMPORTANT.

485

A KING MUST UNDERSTAND THE ACT OF LOVING IS THE
GENERATION OF THE MOST POWERFUL FORCE IN THE
UNIVERSE.

486

A KING MUST UNDERSTAND IF SOMETHING NOBLE MUST
BE DONE OR SAID, NEVER JUDGE YOURSELF UNWORTHY OF
DOING OR SAYING IT.

487

A KING MUST UNDERSTAND IT IS YOUR COURAGE AND
AUDACITY THAT SHALL SEPARATE YOU FROM THE TIMID
MASSES.

488

A KING MUST UNDERSTAND THE STRENGTH OF A MAN'S COURAGE SHOWS BEST DURING HIS HOUR OF ADVERSITY.

489

A KING MUST UNDERSTAND A SILENT TONGUE SHALL NEVER BETRAY HE WHO POSSESSES IT.

490

A KING MUST UNDERSTAND PITY SHALL NOT GET YOU AID. HOWEVER, ADMIRATION AT YOUR REFUSAL TO GIVE IN SHALL.

491

A KING MUST UNDERSTAND WHEN DEALING WITH LIARS, EVEN AN HONEST MAN MUST LIE AT TIMES.

492

A KING MUST UNDERSTAND IF YOU ARE TOLD OR YOU HEAR THAT SOMEONE SPEAKS ILL OF YOU, REALIZE THAT THIS IS ALL THAT HAS HAPPENED AND YOU ARE NOT INJURED IN

493

A KING MUST UNDERSTAND ALL DISTINCTION MUST PAY THE TAX OF ENVY.

494

A KING MUST UNDERSTAND IN ORDER TO INSPIRE RESPECT, YOU MUST FIRST RESPECT YOURSELF.

495

A KING MUST UNDERSTAND THE TENDER AND GENTLE SOULS OF LADIES ARE VERY SUSCEPTIBLE TO HARMONY AND SWEETNESS.

496

A KING MUST UNDERSTAND IF YOU SPEAK WISELY, YOU SHALL GET AHEAD IN THE WORLD. FOR INFLUENTIAL PEOPLE APPRECIATE GOOD SENSE.

497

A KING MUST UNDERSTAND THE GREATEST GIFT THAT

YOU CAN GIVE IS LOVE.

498

A KING MUST UNDERSTAND WISDOM IS ONLY A

COMPANION TO THOSE WHO ARE TRANQUIL IN SPIRIT.

499

A KING MUST UNDERSTAND WITHOUT FAIL, THOSE WHO

HAVE BECOME TRULY GREAT HAVE OFFERED LOVING SERVICE

IN AN UNINTERRUPTED FASHION.

500

A KING MUST UNDERSTAND GREAT CALM IN A MAN

BESPEAKS GREAT STRENGTH IN A MAN.

501

A KING MUST UNDERSTAND THERE IS NONE SO BRAVE

THAT THEY ARE NOT DISTURBED BY SOMETHING

UNEXPECTED.

502

A KING MUST UNDERSTAND WHILE LIFE IS INDEED TO BE

CONQUERED, IT SHALL ONLY YIELD TO VIRTUOUS FORCES.

503

A KING MUST UNDERSTAND IT SHALL NEVER BE POSSIBLE FOR YOU TO BE FINISHED LEARNING. ESPECIALLY IF YOUR PURPOSE IS ABOVE AVERAGE.

504

A KING MUST UNDERSTAND THE TRUTH IS BEYOND ALL BELIEFS.

505

A KING MUST UNDERSTAND IT IS THE NATURE OF MAN NEVER TO BE SATISFIED. FOR AS SOON AS HE IS POSSESSED OF WHAT WITH GREAT VEHEMENCE HE DESIRED, HE WISHES AS FIERCELY FOR SOMETHING ELSE.

506

A KING MUST UNDERSTAND WHEN WAR IS BROUGHT TO YOU, IF YOU DO NOT MAKE WAR LIKE YOUR ENEMY HAS NEVER IMAGINED, EVEN IN THEIR WORST NIGHTMARE, YOU SHALL HAND VICTORY TO YOUR FOE.

507

A KING MUST UNDERSTAND PEACE IS THE KEY TO THE LOCKED DOORS OF **WISDOM, POWER,** AND HAPPINESS.

508

A KING MUST UNDERSTAND INSECURITY IS THE FATHER OF ALL SUSPICION.

509

A KING MUST UNDERSTAND WHEN YOU ASSUME THE APPEARANCE OF **POWER,** PEOPLE SHALL SOON GIVE IT TO YOU.

510

A KING MUST UNDERSTAND NO MATTER HOW ARDUOUS THE JOURNEY THAT DESTINY SENDS HIM ON, A TRUE **KING** SHALL ALWAYS RETURN GREATER THAN WHEN HE LEFT.

511

A KING MUST UNDERSTAND ALL OF YOUR ACTS, YOUR FOLLOWERS SHALL IMITATE. FOR IT IS UPON YOU THAT THEIR EYES LIE.

512

A KING MUST UNDERSTAND WORDS ARE SACRED. THUS,
YOU MUST NEVER LET THEM OUT EASILY.

513

A KING MUST UNDERSTAND YOU MUST DO NOTHING
WITHOUT REGARD TO THE CONSEQUENCES.

514

A KING MUST UNDERSTAND THE ONE PERSON WHO A
KING MUST BE ABLE TO DEPEND UPON, WITHOUT FAIL,
AND WITHOUT DISAPPOINTMENT IN TIMES OF ADVERSITY IS
HIMSELF.

515

A KING MUST UNDERSTAND AN INTELLIGENT KING
WOULD NEVER MAKE STUPID THREATS.

516

A KING MUST UNDERSTAND HE WHO IS NOT OPEN TO
CRITICISM IS NOT OPEN TO IMPROVEMENT.

517

A KING MUST UNDERSTAND NONCHALANCE IS THE MARK OF A **KING**.

518

A **KING** MUST UNDERSTAND IT IS NOT THE ACTIONS OF ANOTHER WHICH BOTHER YOU. RATHER, IT IS YOUR JUDGMENTS CONCERNING THOSE ACTS.

519

A **KING** MUST UNDERSTAND THERE IS NOTHING SO UNCERTAIN AND SO UNSTABLE AS FAME OR **POWER** NOT FOUNDED UPON ITS OWN **STRENGTH**.

520

A **KING** MUST UNDERSTAND **DIGNITY** IS INVARIABLY THE MASK THAT A **KING** MUST DON UNDER ALL CIRCUMSTANCES.

521

A **KING** MUST UNDERSTAND ABOVE ALL ELSE, A HEART IS STIRRED BY THE FEELING THAT IT IS LOVED.

522

A KING MUST UNDERSTAND AN IGNORANT MAN HAS NEVER EVEN THOUGHT ABOUT THOSE THINGS OF WHICH HE IS THE MOST SURE.

523

A KING MUST UNDERSTAND IN ORDER TO ATTRACT **LOVE,** YOU MUST FIRST SEE YOURSELF AS LOVABLE.

524

A KING MUST UNDERSTAND **KNOWLEDGE** IS THE MATERIAL WHICH YOUR ATTENTION USES TO CONSTRUCT YOUR KINGDOM.

525

A KING MUST UNDERSTAND TO BE GREAT YOU MUST SOAR PAST YOUR FEARS OF BOTH FAILURE AND SUCCESS.

526

A KING MUST UNDERSTAND ELEGANCE AND STYLE SHALL WIN OUT OVER VULGARITY ON EVERY OCCASION.

527

A KING MUST UNDERSTAND GROWING OLDER IS SIMPLY THE MEANS BY WHICH ONE ACCUMULATES GREATER **WISDOM** AND **UNDERSTANDING**.

528

A KING MUST UNDERSTAND IN WAR, VICTORY IS NOT GAINED BY THE NUMBER KILLED, BUT BY THE NUMBER FRIGHTENED.

529

A KING MUST UNDERSTAND COURAGE IS ALWAYS THE BEST DEFENSE AGAINST ANY EVIL.

530

A KING MUST UNDERSTAND NO MAN SHALL EVER BE TRULY FREE UNTIL HE LEARNS TO DO HIS OWN THINKING, AND GAINS THE COURAGE TO ACT ON HIS OWN INITIATIVE.

531

A KING MUST UNDERSTAND TIME IS THE FATHER OF ALL TRUTHS.

532

A KING MUST UNDERSTAND THE COMMON MAN IS SELDOM ABLE TO DISCERN MATTERS OF THE SPIRIT BECAUSE THEY ARE FOOLISHNESS TO HIM.

533

A KING MUST UNDERSTAND PEACE IS A HEAVIER BURDEN FOR SLAVES THAN WAR IS FOR THOSE THAT ARE FREE.

534

A KING MUST UNDERSTAND A KING'S PRESENCE EXUDES SUCH A SENSE OF CALMNESS THAT THOSE AROUND HIM ARE ALWAYS LEFT FEELING MORE AT PEACE, LESS THREATENED, AND GENTLY ASSURED.

535

A KING MUST UNDERSTAND NOT ONLY DO PEOPLE DESIRE TO BE ENTERTAINED, IT IS ONE OF THEIR GREATEST NEEDS.

536

A KING MUST UNDERSTAND NO ONE EVER SEIZES POWER WITH THE INTENTION OF LETTING IT GO.

537

A KING MUST UNDERSTAND YOUR PEOPLE SHALL FOLLOW YOU ANYWHERE AS LONG AS YOU REWARD THEM WITH HOPE.

538

A KING MUST UNDERSTAND A KING MUST BE A MASTER OF POWER. HE MUST NEVER ALLOW POWER TO MASTER HIM.

539

A KING MUST UNDERSTAND JUST AS ANY TOOL, INSTRUMENT, OR VESSEL CAN ONLY BE CONSIDERED GOOD IF IT PERFORMS WELL THAT TASK FOR WHICH IT WAS MADE, SO TOO CAN A KING ONLY BE CONSIDERED GOOD IF HE PERFORMS WELL THAT FUNCTION FOR WHICH HE WAS MADE.

540

A KING MUST UNDERSTAND A KING SHOULD ALWAYS KEEP THE FULL EXTENT OF HIS ABILITIES UNKNOWN.

541

A KING MUST UNDERSTAND TIME CONTINUES ON IN

542

A KING MUST UNDERSTAND YOU SHALL ALWAYS BE REWARDED FOR THOSE ACTIONS THAT REVEAL A SENSE OF SELF-SACRIFICE AND DEVOTION.

543

A KING MUST UNDERSTAND IT IS THE WAITING PERIOD OF NIGHT THAT CAUSES ONE TO APPRECIATE THE SUNLIGHT.

544

A KING MUST UNDERSTAND WHEN GRACE IS THE ADORNMENT THAT INFORMS AND ACCOMPANIES ALL OF YOUR ACTIONS, IT SHALL SOON BECOME CLEAR TO ALL THAT YOU ARE WORTHY OF THE COMPANIONSHIP AND FAVOR OF THE GREAT.

545

A KING MUST UNDERSTAND JOY ARRIVES ON THE HEELS OF SORROW.

546

A KING MUST UNDERSTAND THE HEARTS OF THE GREAT
ARE ALWAYS CAPABLE OF CHANGE.

547

A KING MUST UNDERSTAND IT IS NO DISGRACE FOR A
KING TO APPEASE A MAN WHEN IT WAS THE KING
HIMSELF WHO WAS THE FIRST TO GIVE OFFENSE.

548

A KING MUST UNDERSTAND IF THE TREACHEROUS
BETRAYAL OF AN ENEMY CAN BE PROPERLY HELD TO BE A
HATEFUL AND DETESTABLE CRIME, CONSIDER HOW MUCH
WORSE AN OFFENCE IS THE BETRAYAL OF THE WOMAN THAT IS
IN LOVE WITH YOU.

549

A KING MUST UNDERSTAND ATTEMPTING TO GIVE
WISDOM TO A FOOL IS LIKE TRYING TO AWAKEN A
DRUNK MAN FROM A DEEP SLEEP.

550

A KING MUST UNDERSTAND WHEN YOU GIVE OF YOURSELF WITH LOVE, YOU LOSE NOTHING.

551

A KING MUST UNDERSTAND ALL OF THE CONFLICTS THAT EXIST IN YOUR KINGDOM ARE DUE TO A LACK OF RESPECT.

552

A KING MUST UNDERSTAND DOUBT IS A TRAITOR THAT SHALL CAUSE YOU TO LOSE WHATEVER GOOD YOU MIGHT HAVE GAINED BY CAUSING YOU TO BE AFRAID EVEN TO MAKE AN ATTEMPT.

553

A KING MUST UNDERSTAND KNOWLEDGE WITHOUT ACTION IS VAIN, UNIMPORTANT, AND FRUITLESS.

554

A KING MUST UNDERSTAND THERE IS NO FATE WORSE THAN CONTINUALLY LIVING IN FEAR.

555

A KING MUST UNDERSTAND THERE IS NOTHING THAT SHOULD BE MORE NATURALLY DESIRED BY YOU THAN **KNOWLEDGE**.

556

A KING MUST UNDERSTAND IF YOU WOULD CONTROL YOUR OWN MIND, YOUR KINGDOM SHALL NEVER BE CONTROLLED BY THE MINDS OF OTHERS.

557

A KING MUST UNDERSTAND **THE TRUTH** IS THE FORCE THAT ALLOWS THE UNIVERSE TO MOVE.

558

A KING MUST UNDERSTAND THE NATURE OF THE MASSES IS AS FICKLE AS THE WIND. WHILE IT MAY BE EASY TO PERSUADE THEM, IT IS AN EXCEEDINGLY DIFFICULT TASK TO FIX THEM IN THAT PERSUASION.

559

A KING MUST UNDERSTAND THE ACTIONS OF ALL MEN ARE

560

A KING MUST UNDERSTAND ANYONE CAN LEAD A FIGHT AFTER IT IS DONE. IT IS LEADING A FIGHT DURING THE FIGHT THAT MAKES ONE A KING.

561

A KING MUST UNDERSTAND THE ONLY MAN WILLING TO DISTURB THE PEACE OF OTHERS IS ONE WHO IS NOT AT PEACE.

562

A KING MUST UNDERSTAND SELF-PITY IS NOTHING MORE THAN AN ALIBI FOR A LACK OF AMBITION.

563

A KING MUST UNDERSTAND IT IS THE FEAR OF LOSING POWER THAT CORRUPTS THOSE THAT HAVE IT.

564

A KING MUST UNDERSTAND IF YOU ARE TOO FORGIVING

WITH A TRANSGRESSOR, YOU SHALL INJURE THE INNOCENT.

565

A KING MUST UNDERSTAND WITHOUT LOVE, POWER MAKES A MAN MORE LIKE AN ANIMAL THAN THE DIVINE.

566

A KING MUST UNDERSTAND GOOD IMPULSES DIE FOR A LACK OF BEING ACTED UPON.

567

A KING MUST UNDERSTAND WHEN YOU ARE TEMPTED TO REVEAL HOW CLEVER YOU ARE, REMEMBER THAT IT IS FAR MORE CLEVER TO CONCEAL THE EXTENT OF ONE'S CLEVERNESS.

568

A KING MUST UNDERSTAND YOU SHALL BE TESTED FOR SOUND CHARACTER, NOT ONLY THROUGH YOUR HOURS OF GREAT ADVERSITY, BUT ALSO DURING YOUR TIMES OF GREAT VICTORY AND MATERIAL SUCCESS.

569

A KING MUST UNDERSTAND IT IS BY SHOWING A CALM, UNRUFFLED EXTERIOR IN THE FACE OF UNPLEASANTNESS THAT YOU SHALL PUT YOUR PEOPLE AT EASE.

570

A KING MUST UNDERSTAND ONE LEARNS OBEDIENCE AND HUMILITY FROM WHAT ONE SUFFERS.

571

A KING MUST UNDERSTAND HE WHO BEHAVES WITH GRACE SHALL FIND IT IN OTHERS ALSO.

572

A KING MUST UNDERSTAND EVERY GLORIOUS REIGN HAS HAD DARK PATCHES DURING WHICH THE CROWN HAS BEEN UNPOPULAR.

573

A KING MUST UNDERSTAND THERE IS GREAT RISK INVOLVED IN ALL ACTIONS THAT ARE TAKEN TO SECURE HONOR.

574

A KING MUST UNDERSTAND IT IS YOUR DISCIPLINE AND COMMITMENT TO ACHIEVING EXCELLENCE THAT SHALL DISTINGUISH YOU FROM COMMON MEN.

575

A KING MUST UNDERSTAND MUCH IS LACKING TO THE KING WHO LACKS THE BEAUTY OF GOODNESS IN HIS HEART.

576

A KING MUST UNDERSTAND JUST AS PRAISE ADDS NOTHING TO THE BEAUTY OF A DIAMOND, MAKING IT NEITHER BETTER NOR WORSE, SO TOO SHALL PRAISE NEITHER MAKE YOU BETTER NOR WORSE.

577

A KING MUST UNDERSTAND THERE IS NO FORTUNE WORTH THE PRICE OF TRUE LOVE.

578

A KING MUST UNDERSTAND A KING MUST NEVER ALLOW

THE LIGHT OF HIS **WISDOM** TO BE OVERSHADOWED BY THE DARKNESS OF HIS PRIDE.

579

A **KING** MUST UNDERSTAND FANATICISM IS NOTHING MORE THAN OVERCOMPENSATED DOUBT.

580

A **KING** MUST UNDERSTAND THE PRICE OF GREATNESS IS RESPONSIBILITY.

581

A **KING** MUST UNDERSTAND A MIND FULL OF FEAR HAS NO ROOM LEFT FOR A VISION.

582

A **KING** MUST UNDERSTAND A **KING** MUST STRIVE TO MAKE HIMSELF INTO A MORE THAN AVERAGE SCHOLAR. FOR STUDIES SHALL MAKE ONE WELL-INFORMED, ELOQUENT, SELF-CONFIDENT, AND ASSURED, NO MATTER TO WHOM ONE IS SPEAKING.

583

A KING MUST UNDERSTAND GREAT ACHIEVEMENTS CAN ONLY COME FROM MINDS THAT ARE AT PEACE WITH THEMSELVES.

584

A KING MUST UNDERSTAND YOUR TRUTH IS THE SUM TOTAL OF ALL OF YOUR THOUGHTS, WORDS, AND ACTIONS.

585

A KING MUST UNDERSTAND BECAUSE NO COURSE OF ACTION IS COMPLETELY SAFE, AND ONE CAN NEVER AVOID TROUBLE WITHOUT RUNNING INTO ANOTHER, **WISDOM** CONSISTS IN KNOWING HOW TO DISTINGUISH THE CHARACTER OF TROUBLES, AND CHOOSING THE LESSER EVIL.

586

A KING MUST UNDERSTAND YOU MUST NEVER ALLOW WORDS FROM AN ENEMY TO FRIGHTEN YOU, OR COUNSEL FROM A FRIEND TO DELUDE YOU.

587

A KING MUST UNDERSTAND HE WHOSE HEART IS NOT

GOVERNED BY PEACE SHALL BE RULED BY TURMOIL.

588

A KING MUST UNDERSTAND YOU SHOULD NEVER ATTEMPT

TO REASON WITH AN ANGRY MAN. FOR AN ANGRY MAN IS

TEMPORARILY WITHOUT REASON.

589

A KING MUST UNDERSTAND A KING MUST NEVER ALLOW

SOMEONE ELSE TO DICTATE WHO HE CHOOSES TO BE.

590

A KING MUST UNDERSTAND AFFECTATION IS A DEPLORABLE

VICE THAT SPRINGS FROM ONE'S OVER ANXIETY TO SHOW

HOW MUCH THEY KNOW.

591

A KING MUST UNDERSTAND ALL OF YOUR POWER LIES

IN THE AWARENESS OF THAT POWER. FOR THE SECRET TO

POWER IS THE CONSCIOUSNESS OF IT.

592

A KING MUST UNDERSTAND THE STIFFEST TREE IS THE ONE MOST EASILY CRACKED.

593

A KING MUST UNDERSTAND THE APPEARANCE OF A SYMPATHETIC EAR SHALL ENTICE ANYONE TO TALK.

594

A KING MUST UNDERSTAND THE MEASURE OF YOUR SUCCESS SHALL BE IN EXACT PROPORTION TO THE SCOPE OF THE ADVERSITY THAT YOU HAVE EXPERIENCED AND MASTERED.

595

A KING MUST UNDERSTAND ANY FOOL CAN MAKE A PROMISE. WHAT SETS A KING APART IS HIS ABILITY TO DELIVER ON HIS PROMISES.

596

A KING MUST UNDERSTAND WHEN THE WORST THAT CAN HAPPEN TO YOU ACTUALLY HAPPENS, AND YOU BEAR IT, YOU

SHALL EMERGE STRONGER THAN YOU EVER IMAGINED.

597

A KING MUST UNDERSTAND A **KING** MUST LEARN TO STEER AWAY FROM AFFECTATION AT ALL COST, FORGO, AND PRACTICE IN ALL THINGS A CERTAIN NONCHALANCE WHICH CONCEALS ALL ARTISTRY AND MAKES WHATEVER HE SAYS OR DOES SEEM UNCONTRIVED AND EFFORTLESS.

598

A KING MUST UNDERSTAND THERE HAS NEVER BEEN A GREAT **KING** THAT HAS HAD AN EASY PAST.

599

A KING MUST UNDERSTAND HE WHO HESITATES FOR BUT A SECOND, PERHAPS ALLOWS TO ESCAPE THAT GIFT WHICH LIFE HELD FOR HIM DURING THAT EXACT MOMENT.

600

A KING MUST UNDERSTAND HE WHO TEACHES LEARNS.

601

A KING MUST UNDERSTAND ONCE THE FLAME OF LOVE

FOR A BEAUTIFUL WOMAN IGNITES WITHIN YOUR HEART,

COWARDICE CAN NEVER POSSESS IT.

602

A KING MUST UNDERSTAND WHEREVER LIFE IS POSSIBLE, IT

IS POSSIBLE TO LIVE VIRTUOUSLY.

603

A KING MUST UNDERSTAND WHERE FEAR REIGNS, THERE IS

NO LOVE.

604

A KING MUST UNDERSTAND TO HAVE ALL THE

KNOWLEDGE IN THE WORLD IS USELESS IF YOU HAVE

NOT THE WISDOM TO APPLY IT IN THE PROPER MANNER.

605

A KING MUST UNDERSTAND A FRIGHTENED MAN SHALL

ALWAYS BE DEFEATED.

606

A KING MUST UNDERSTAND SINCERITY IS A RARE JEWEL THAT IS FOUND ONLY IN THE SOULS OF A SELECT FEW.

607

A KING MUST UNDERSTAND FEAR FED BY GUILT MAKES MEN DO STRANGE THINGS.

608

A KING MUST UNDERSTAND IT IS MORE FITTING FOR A **KING** TO BE EDUCATED THAN ANYONE ELSE.

609

A KING MUST UNDERSTAND YOUR MIND SHALL ALWAYS CREATE EXCELLENT IDEAS AS LONG AS YOU DO NOT KEEP IT TOO OCCUPIED WITH TERRIBLE THOUGHTS.

610

A KING MUST UNDERSTAND **THE TRUTH** SPEAKS LOUDER THAN WORDS.

611

A KING MUST UNDERSTAND AS AN ACORN GROWS INTO AN OAK TREE, SO TOO DO GREAT MEN GROW INTO THEIR GREATNESS.

612

A KING MUST UNDERSTAND THERE IS NO VICTORY THAT IS EVER SO COMPLETE THAT THE VICTOR MUST NOT SHOW REGARD TO JUSTICE.

613

A KING MUST UNDERSTAND WITHOUT AN INFLUENCE OF PEACE, NO PRODUCTIVE CHANGE CAN OCCUR.

614

A KING MUST UNDERSTAND LIFE SHALL YIELD ITS MOST PROFOUND SECRETS TO THE KING THAT IS DETERMINED TO UNCOVER THEM.

615

A KING MUST UNDERSTAND TO ACHIEVE SELF-MASTERY IS TO BECOME THE MASTER OF EVERYTHING.

616

A KING MUST UNDERSTAND GREAT AGE IMPARTS
DIGNITY NOT ONLY TO BUILDINGS, STATUES, AND
PICTURES, BUT TO EVERYTHING THAT IS ABLE TO WITHSTAND
THE TEST OF TIME.

617

A KING MUST UNDERSTAND THE MORE ONE IS IMPRESSED
BY POWER, THE EASIER THEY ARE TO COMMAND.

618

A KING MUST UNDERSTAND IT IS A GRAVE ERROR FOR A
KING TO BECOME OVERSENSITIVE IN THE FACE OF
CRITICISM.

619

A KING MUST UNDERSTAND IT IS FAR EASIER TO RUN INTO
DANGER WHEN ONE SWIMS AGAINST THE CURRENT OF THE
RIVER RATHER THAN WITH IT.

620

A KING MUST UNDERSTAND EVERY SOUL IS REBORN WHEN

621

A KING MUST UNDERSTAND A KING MUST NEVER ALLOW HIS EYES TO SHOW FEAR OR NERVES, EVEN IF HE FEELS THESE THINGS INSIDE OF HIMSELF.

622

A KING MUST UNDERSTAND IT IS OUT OF THE ASHES OF THE PAST THAT NEW LIFE IS BEGUN.

623

A KING MUST UNDERSTAND WHENEVER AN ACTION IS PERFORMED GREATLY WITH NONCHALANCE, IT SHALL CAUSE THE PERSON TO APPEAR TO HAVE EVEN GREATER SKILL THAN HE ACTUALLY POSSESSES.

624

A KING MUST UNDERSTAND ALL THAT COMES FROM THE EARTH IS ONLY DUST.

625

A KING MUST UNDERSTAND EVEN THE HARDEST STONE

CAN BE WORN DOWN WITH ENOUGH RAIN.

626

A KING MUST UNDERSTAND IN ORDER TO BE KING,

YOUR ENTIRE MANNER MUST GIVE EVIDENCE TO THAT

CALMNESS AND RESOLUTION PECULIAR TO THOSE WHO ARE

ACCUSTOMED TO FACING THEIR FEARS.

627

A KING MUST UNDERSTAND HE WHO LOVES A LOT, SAYS

ONLY A LITTLE.

628

A KING MUST UNDERSTAND A KING, IN ANY SITUATION

THAT HE FINDS HIMSELF IN, MUST CONTROL NOT ONLY HIS

WORDS, BUT EVEN THE EXPRESSIONS ON HIS FACE.

629

A KING MUST UNDERSTAND THE GREATER THE

CONVICTION WITH WHICH YOU LOVE, THE MORE LOVE

630

A KING MUST UNDERSTAND THE KING WHO LACKS WISDOM SHALL USE HIS KNOWLEDGE AS A WEAPON TO DESTROY, WHILE THE WISE KING SHALL USE HIS KNOWLEDGE AS A TOOL TO BUILD.

631

A KING MUST UNDERSTAND HE WHO FREEZES UP IN A BATTLE SHOWS THE WORLD THAT HE HAS ALLOWED FEAR TO ROB HIM OF BOTH HIS WIT AND HIS SKILL.

632

A KING MUST UNDERSTAND HE WHO WORSHIPS DIVINE PATIENCE SHALL ALWAYS HAVE TIME AS AN ALLY.

633

A KING MUST UNDERSTAND MEN SHALL GO TO FAR GREATER LENGTHS TO AVOID WHAT THEY FEAR THAN TO OBTAIN WHAT THEY DESIRE.

634

A KING MUST UNDERSTAND IN TIMES PAST, JUST AS THE WORLD HAD NOT MEN WHO WERE AS EVIL AS THEY ARE TODAY, THEY HAD NOT MEN WHO ARE AS VIRTUOUS. FOR BECAUSE, FOR THE MOST PART, PRESENT TIMES PRODUCE MEN WHO ARE MUCH MORE CAPABLE THAN IN THE PAST. THOSE WHO TURN TO GOOD DO FAR BETTER THAN THEY DID IN THE PAST, JUST AS THOSE WHO TURN TO EVIL DO FAR WORSE.

635

A KING MUST UNDERSTAND YOU SHALL BE ABLE TO CONTROL YOUR DESTINY TO THE EXTENT THAT YOU ARE ABLE TO CONTROL YOUR MIND.

636

A KING MUST UNDERSTAND ALTHOUGH MANY START OFF DOWN A FALSE PATH TO THEIR TRUE DESTINY, TIME AND FORTUNE USUALLY CORRECT THEIR STEPS AND SET THEM ARIGHT.

637

A KING MUST UNDERSTAND HE WHO IS NOT A FATHER TO

HIS CHILDREN CAN NEVER BE A TRUE **KING**.

638

A KING MUST UNDERSTAND GREATNESS SHALL NEVER BE

ATTAINED WITHOUT INNER HARMONY AND PEACE.

639

A KING MUST UNDERSTAND THE WORSE FATE IN THE

WORLD FOR THE MAN WHO YEARNS FOR FAME, GLORY, OR

POWER IS TO BE IGNORED.

640

A KING MUST UNDERSTAND BY CONTROLLING YOURSELF,

YOU CONTROL THE ENTIRE WORLD.

641

A KING MUST UNDERSTAND IN ORDER TO SPEAK OR WRITE

WELL, IT IS ESSENTIAL THAT YOU POSSESS **KNOWLEDGE**.

FOR HE WHO LACKS **KNOWLEDGE** HAS NOTHING IN

HIS MIND WORTH HEARING, AND THUS NOTHING WORTH

WRITING OR SPEAKING.

642

A KING MUST UNDERSTAND POWER RESIDES WHEREVER

YOU BELIEVE THAT IT DOES.

643

A KING MUST UNDERSTAND THOSE WHO UNDERSTAND

WELL HOW TO FOLLOW SHALL ONE DAY COME TO COMMAND.

644

A KING MUST UNDERSTAND THE MOST ESSENTIAL

COMPONENT OF GAINING POWER IS SELF-DISCIPLINE.

645

A KING MUST UNDERSTAND WITHOUT A WORTHY

OPPONENT, ONE SHALL NEVER GROW STRONGER.

646

A KING MUST UNDERSTAND BECAUSE SURPRISES CAUSE ONE

TO BECOME EMOTIONAL AND WEAK, YOU YOURSELF MUST

ALWAYS BE SURPRISING AND NEVER SURPRISED BY ANYTHING.

647

A KING MUST UNDERSTAND BEHIND EVERY DARK

HAPPENING AND DIFFICULTY LIE A HIDDEN BLESSING.

648

A KING MUST UNDERSTAND IN ORDER FOR A **KING** TO

BE CONSIDERED EXCELLENT, IT IS ESSENTIAL THAT HE KNOWS

HOW TO BOTH SPEAK AND WRITE WELL.

649

A KING MUST UNDERSTAND IN SPEECH, LUCIDITY SHALL

ALWAYS WALK HAND IN HAND WITH EXCELLENCE.

650

A KING MUST UNDERSTAND OPPOSITION IS THE FUEL OF

CREATIVITY.

651

A KING MUST UNDERSTAND AS LONG AS YOU KEEP YOUR

DESTINY IN THE FOREFRONT OF YOUR THOUGHTS, EVERY

MOMENT IN LIFE SHALL PROVIDE YOU WITH AN OPPORTUNITY

TO MOVE CLOSER TO IT.

652

A KING **MUST UNDERSTAND** IF YOU WISH TO ACCOMPLISH SOME GREAT THING IN THIS LIFE, YOU MUST APPLY YOURSELF TO WORK WITH SUCH A DEDICATION THAT TO IDLE SPECTATORS WHO LIVE ONLY TO AMUSE THEMSELVES, YOUR DEDICATION APPEARS TO BE INSANITY.

653

A KING **MUST UNDERSTAND** MEN CAN DISPLAY THEIR AFFECTION WITH FAR LESS RISK THAN WOMEN.

654

A KING **MUST UNDERSTAND** NEGATIVITY IS NEVER INTELLIGENT.

655

A KING **MUST UNDERSTAND** GOOD KINGS UNDERSTAND THAT IT IS BETTER TO RULE WITH THE HEART THAN WITH THE SWORD.

656

A KING **MUST UNDERSTAND** THE WAY A PERSON USES

THEIR WORDS IS THE TELLING FACTOR IN HOW THEY SHALL

USE THEIR **KNOWLEDGE**.

657

A **KING** MUST UNDERSTAND DOUBT AND FEAR ARE THE

ARCHENEMIES OF **KNOWLEDGE**.

658

A **KING** MUST UNDERSTAND THE COMPASSION OF THE

KING RULES THE FATE OF HIS PEOPLE.

659

A **KING** MUST UNDERSTAND THERE IS **WISDOM** FOUND

IN EVERY WOUND.

660

A **KING** MUST UNDERSTAND NO GOOD EVER CAME FROM

DESPAIR, NOR FROM DWELLING UPON THE NEGATIVE SIDE OF

ANY SITUATION.

661

A **KING** MUST UNDERSTAND ALL DARKNESS FLEES FROM

662

A KING MUST UNDERSTAND IT IS THOSE WHO ARE BELIEVED TO BE BOTH WORTHY AND MODEST THAT ARE ESTEEMED THE HIGHEST.

663

A KING MUST UNDERSTAND IN ALL OF YOUR DAYS, YOU MUST SEEK UNDERSTANDING. FOR IT IS A TERRIBLE THING WHEN THOSE WHO MUST BE GOVERNED ARE WISER THAN THE RULERS WHO MUST GOVERN THEM.

664

A KING MUST UNDERSTAND GENIUS LIES NOT IN THE EXTENSITY OF ONE'S KNOWLEDGE, BUT IN THE INTENSITY.

665

A KING MUST UNDERSTAND IN WAR, THE MAN WITH SUPERIOR INTELLIGENCE AND ORGANIZATION SHALL ALWAYS BE THE VICTOR.

666

A KING MUST UNDERSTAND IT IS ONLY WHEN YOU HAVE PREPARED YOURSELF FOR WAR THAT YOU CAN TRULY HAVE PEACE.

667

A KING MUST UNDERSTAND YOU SHALL GAIN THE STRENGTH OF EVERY TEMPTATION THAT YOU ARE ABLE TO RESIST.

668

A KING MUST UNDERSTAND ONCE YOU HAVE DECIDED SOMETHING ABOUT YOURSELF, EVERYTHING IN THE OUTSIDE WORLD MUST CONFORM TO THAT DECISION.

669

A KING MUST UNDERSTAND THE MOST CONVINCING PROOF OF WHETHER A MAN UNDERSTANDS SOMETHING LIES IN HIS ABILITY TO TEACH IT.

670

A KING MUST UNDERSTAND THE MAN WHO KNOWS HOW

TO COMMAND SHALL ALWAYS BE OBEYED.

671

A KING MUST UNDERSTAND A WISE KING SHALL NEVER GIVE A HUNGRY MAN REASON TO RESENT HIM.

672

A KING MUST UNDERSTAND THE USE OF FORCE AS A MEANS OF COERCION SHALL ONLY STRENGTHEN PEOPLE'S RESISTANCE TO YOUR INFLUENCE.

673

A KING MUST UNDERSTAND A WISE KING PROFITS MORE FROM HIS ENEMIES THAN A FOOL DOES FROM HIS FRIENDS.

674

A KING MUST UNDERSTAND EMOTIONAL PEOPLE ARE EASY TO DECEIVE, THEREFORE YOU MUST BECOME A MASTER OF YOUR EMOTIONS.

675

A KING MUST UNDERSTAND THE GREATEST THREAT TO

676

A KING MUST UNDERSTAND ONLY THE WEAKEST REEDS ARE

FLATTENED BY THE WIND.

677

A KING MUST UNDERSTAND MEN ARE ONLY EQUAL WHEN

THEY HAVE EQUAL CONFIDENCE.

678

A KING MUST UNDERSTAND WHEN YOU ARE WORTHY AND

PEOPLE BELIEVE THAT YOU ARE AVERSE TO USURPING

AUTHORITY OVER THEM, THEY SHALL GROW THE READIER TO

SURRENDER THEMSELVES INTO YOUR HANDS.

679

A KING MUST UNDERSTAND THE BEST WAY TO WIN FAVOR

FROM LADIES IS TO SERVE AND PLEASE THEM.

680

A KING MUST UNDERSTAND MORE THAN ANYONE ELSE, YOU MUST BE KIND TO UNKIND PEOPLE. FOR THEY ARE THE ONES WHO NEED IT THE MOST.

681

A KING MUST UNDERSTAND ONE LEARNS A GREAT DEAL ABOUT THE TRUE NATURE OF A PERSON BY OBSERVING THE WAY THAT THEY LOVE, WHY THEY LOVE, AND WHAT THEY LOVE.

682

A KING MUST UNDERSTAND SILENCE IS THE LANGUAGE OF THE DIVINE.

683

A KING MUST UNDERSTAND FEAR HAS NO PLACE IN THE DECISIONS OF AN ORDERED MIND.

684

A KING MUST UNDERSTAND NERVOUSNESS IS MERELY ENERGY MIXED WITH FEARFUL THOUGHTS.

685

A KING MUST UNDERSTAND WHAT YOU THINK OF YOURSELF IS REFLECTED IN HOW YOU CARRY YOURSELF.

686

A KING MUST UNDERSTAND THE DREAMS OF FUTURE KINGDOMS OFTEN BEGIN SITTING AROUND TALKING TO DEAR FRIENDS.

687

A KING MUST UNDERSTAND FREEDOM FROM INNER CONFLICT, THE VERY DEFINITION OF INNER PEACE, IS THE HIGHEST FREEDOM THAT THERE IS.

688

A KING MUST UNDERSTAND JUST BECAUSE SOMETHING IS NOT LIKELY TO HAPPEN, YOU MUST NEVER MAKE THE MISTAKE OF ASSUMING THAT IT SHALL NEVER HAPPEN.

689

A KING MUST UNDERSTAND IN THE CASE OF ALL THOSE WHO LIVE, THE POWER THAT CREATED THEM REMAINS

690

A KING MUST UNDERSTAND FLATTERY IS LIKE THE VOICE OF THE SIRENS THAT CAUSE SHIPWRECK TO ALL THOSE WHO DO NOT STOP THEIR EARS TO ITS DECEPTIVE HARMONY.

691

A KING MUST UNDERSTAND THE FARTHER YOUR VISION EXTENDS AND THE MORE STEPS YOU PLAN AHEAD, THE MORE POWERFUL YOU SHALL BECOME.

692

A KING MUST UNDERSTAND ARGUING WITH THE LOQUACIOUS IS LIKE THROWING DRY TIMBER ON A FIRE.

693

A KING MUST UNDERSTAND IF A PERSON EXPECTS PAIN AND YOU GIVE THEM PLEASURE INSTEAD, YOU SHALL HAVE WON THE BATTLE FOR THEIR HEART IN THAT VERY INSTANT.

694

A KING MUST UNDERSTAND YOU MUST ALWAYS STRIVE TO ENDEAR YOURSELF TO EVEN THOSE WHO HOLD THE LOWLIEST POSITION IN YOUR KINGDOM. FOR THE WIDER YOUR SUPPORT BASE, THE STRONGER SHALL BE YOUR **POWER**.

695

A KING MUST UNDERSTAND A GOOD WORD CONCERNING SOMEONE WHO SPEAKS EVIL OF YOU IS THE ONLY ACCEPTABLE RESPONSE FOR A **KING**.

696

A KING MUST UNDERSTAND IT IS THE WISE **KING** WHO STRIVES TO SEE THE WORLD FROM THE STANDPOINT OF HIS ASSAILANTS. FOR IT IS MORE IN HIS INTEREST THAN IT IS THEIRS TO LOCATE HIS WEAKNESSES.

697

A KING MUST UNDERSTAND YOU CAN PROMOTE YOURSELF TO ANY POSITION THAT YOU DESIRE SIMPLY BY PREPARING YOURSELF TO BE ABLE TO DO WHAT THAT POSITION REQUIRES.

698

A KING MUST UNDERSTAND NEITHER THE MAN WHO CANNOT DO WHAT HE IS TOLD, NOR THE MAN WHO CAN DO NOTHING BESIDES WHAT HE IS TOLD SHALL EVER BECOME KING.

699

A KING MUST UNDERSTAND YOUR PERSONALITY SHALL BE EITHER YOUR GREATEST ASSET OR YOUR GREATEST LIABILITY.

700

A KING MUST UNDERSTAND EVERY WORD THAT YOU SPEAK LEAVES ITS IMPRINT UPON YOUR MIND AND BECOMES A PART OF YOUR PERSONALITY.

701

A KING MUST UNDERSTAND A KING'S GREATNESS IS SHOWN IN HIS RESPONSE TO ADVERSITY.

702

A KING MUST UNDERSTAND EVERY STORM RUNS OUT OF RAIN EVENTUALLY.

703

A KING MUST UNDERSTAND COURAGE AND FAITH ARE

YOUR BEST PROTECTION WHEN YOU ARE THREATENED WITH

DOOM.

704

A KING MUST UNDERSTAND IF YOU GAIN THE

CONFIDENCE OF A MAN WHEN HE IS DOWN, YOU SHALL

SHARE IN HIS HAPPINESS IF HE BECOMES SUCCESSFUL. YOU

MUST STAND BY A MAN WHEN HE IS IN TROUBLE IF YOU

WANT TO STAND WITH HIM WHEN BETTER TIMES COME HIS

WAY.

705

A KING MUST UNDERSTAND A MAN IS ONLY RESPECTED

WHEN HE IS EITHER A TRUE FRIEND OR A DOWNRIGHT

ENEMY.

706

A KING MUST UNDERSTAND A MAN WHO IS NOT WISE

SHALL NEVER TAKE GOOD ADVICE.

707

A KING MUST UNDERSTAND EXCELLENCE IS ALWAYS
ADMIRED, EVEN BY ITS ENEMIES.

708

A KING MUST UNDERSTAND BECAUSE KINGS ADD TO
THEIR SOCIETY IN WAYS THAT DEFINE THE LIVES OF THEIR
DESCENDANTS, EVERY DEED THAT YOU PERFORM, YOU MUST
PERFORM WITH THIS IN THE FORE OF YOUR MIND.

709

A KING MUST UNDERSTAND OSTENTATION AND POMP
SEEN ON A DAILY BASIS SHALL CONTRACT MORE ENVY THAN
GRAVITY AND MODERATION.

710

A KING MUST UNDERSTAND IN YOUR DISCOURSES WITH
OTHERS, YOU MUST BE ELOQUENT AND FACETIOUS, IN YOUR
RESOLUTIONS, WISE, AND IN YOUR EXECUTIONS, QUICK AND
COURAGEOUS.

711

A KING MUST UNDERSTAND IN ORDER TO BRING SUCCESS AND **HONOR** TO YOURSELF, YOU MUST DO RIGHT AND STUDY. FOR OTHERS SHALL HELP YOU IF YOU WOULD BUT HELP YOURSELF.

712

A KING MUST UNDERSTAND IF YOU DESIRE TO BE LOVED BY A WOMAN, YOU YOURSELF MUST **LOVE** AND BE LOVABLE.

713

A KING MUST UNDERSTAND CURIOSITY IS THE BEST SEEKER OF **KNOWLEDGE**.

714

A KING MUST UNDERSTAND IF YOU GIVE A WOMAN FRUSTRATION, SHE SHALL GIVE YOU HELL.

715

A KING MUST UNDERSTAND MONUMENTS OF PRIDE SOON BECOME MEMORIALS OF FOLLY.

716

A KING MUST UNDERSTAND FEAR AND DOUBT ARE LIKE VINES GROWING BETWEEN MORTARED STONES. GIVEN ENOUGH TIME, THEY SHALL DESTROY EVEN THE STRONGEST WALL.

717

A KING MUST UNDERSTAND HE WHO BECOMES DEFENSIVE IS MERELY A PUPPET WHOSE STRINGS ARE BEING PULLED BY DOUBT.

718

A KING MUST UNDERSTAND EVERY THOUGHT THAT YOU HAVE SHALL EITHER HEAL OR HARM.

719

A KING MUST UNDERSTAND ONLY A FOOL CHARGES INTO BATTLE WITHOUT A PLAN.

720

A KING MUST UNDERSTAND IN ORDER TO TRULY KNOW THE TRUTH, YOU MUST BECOME IT.

721

A KING MUST UNDERSTAND THE ABILITY TO FILL THE VOIDS OF PEOPLE'S UNHAPPINESS AND INSECURITY IS AN INFINITE SOURCE OF POWER.

722

A KING MUST UNDERSTAND A TRUE MASTER SHALL ONLY SEEK TO MASTER HIMSELF.

723

A KING MUST UNDERSTAND PAIN AND PLEASURE ARE JOINED END TO END SO THAT THE BEGINNING OF ONE IS ALWAYS THE END OF THE OTHER. FOR ONE IS NEVER ALLOWED PLEASURE WITHOUT PAIN BEFOREHAND.

724

A KING MUST UNDERSTAND IT IS THE NATURAL COURSE OF THINGS THAT A KING SHALL FIND HIMSELF DEALING MORE OFTEN WITH THE COMMON THAN WITH HIS PEERS.

725

A KING MUST UNDERSTAND IGNORANCE OF HOW TO RULE

GIVES RISE TO SO MANY EVILS, SO MUCH DEATH,
DESTRUCTION, PERDITION, AND RUINATION THAT IT MAY BE
SAID THAT IT IS THE DEADLIEST PLAGUE OF ALL.

726

A KING MUST UNDERSTAND THE GREEDIER SOMEONE IS,
THE EASIER THEY CAN BE DECEIVED.

727

A KING MUST UNDERSTAND IT IS A GREAT WRONG TO
REFUSE TO **HONOR** AN INTELLIGENT PERSON SIMPLY
BECAUSE THEY ARE POOR.

728

A KING MUST UNDERSTAND TO REPEAT SECRETS IS TO
HAVE REGRETS.

729

A KING MUST UNDERSTAND YOU SHALL LEARN THE MOST
ABOUT A MAN BY OBSERVING HOW HE BEHAVES WITH HIS
PEERS.

730

A KING MUST UNDERSTAND THERE ARE MANY OBSTACLES AND DIFFICULTIES THAT CANNOT BE OVERCOME IF YOU TRY TO CONQUER THEM ALL AT ONCE. HOWEVER, THEY SHALL ALMOST ALL INVARIABLY YIELD TO YOU IF YOU WOULD MASTER THEM LITTLE BY LITTLE.

731

A KING MUST UNDERSTAND THE HERO OF ANY STORY COULD NOT EXIST WERE IT NOT FOR THE VILLAINS THAT CHALLENGED HIM ALONG HIS PATH.

732

A KING MUST UNDERSTAND JUST AS THE BEAUTIFUL LOTUS FLOWER GROWS OUT OF THE MOST DISGUSTING MUCK, SO TOO CAN THE MOST BEAUTIFUL ATTRIBUTES IN A PERSON ARISE FROM THE MOST PAINFUL OF CIRCUMSTANCES.

733

A KING MUST UNDERSTAND ALTHOUGH YOU MAY NOT GET ALL THAT YOU PAY FOR IN THIS LIFE, YOU MUST CERTAINLY PAY FOR ALL THAT YOU GET.

734

A KING MUST UNDERSTAND THOSE WHO IN TIME OF PERIL ARE INTENT UPON SUPPLYING THEIR OWN WANTS ARE NOT TO BE TRUSTED IN AN EMERGENCY.

735

A KING MUST UNDERSTAND IN THE SCHOOL OF AFFLICTION, PATIENCE IS THE FIRST SUBJECT THAT ONE MUST MASTER.

736

A KING MUST UNDERSTAND GOOD FORTUNE LIES IN THE ABILITY TO HANDLE BAD FORTUNE COURAGEOUSLY.

737

A KING MUST UNDERSTAND YOU MUST NEVER JUDGE ANY EXPERIENCE AS GOOD OR BAD THAT CAN HAPPEN TO BOTH THE GOOD AND THE BAD MAN ALIKE.

738

A KING MUST UNDERSTAND BEFORE MAKING ANY DECLARATION OF LOVE TO A WOMAN, YOU MUST MAKE

SURE THAT YOU DON'T OFFEND HER BY DOING SO. FOR TO OFFEND HER IS TO NOT DECLARE YOUR **LOVE** AT ALL.

739

A KING MUST UNDERSTAND TRUE **LOVE** IS A FIRE THAT SHALL NEVER DIE, FOR IT IS FED ON CONSTANT HOPE.

740

A KING MUST UNDERSTAND IT IS ONLY WHEN **WISDOM** IS UTTERED THAT IT SHALL MAKE ITSELF KNOWN.

741

A KING MUST UNDERSTAND THERE IS NOTHING AT ALL MANLY ABOUT PETULANCE.

742

A KING MUST UNDERSTAND THE PRIDE THAT MAKES A SHOW OF PIETY IS THE MOST PERVERSE PRIDE OF ALL.

743

A KING MUST UNDERSTAND IT IS THE WISE MAN THAT

GLORIFIES PATIENCE AND MISTRUSTS HASTE.

744

A KING MUST UNDERSTAND PATIENCE IS THE ABILITY TO ALLOW THINGS TO UNFOLD IN A MORE MAGNIFICENT WAY THAN YOU ARE ABLE TO FORESEE.

745

A KING MUST UNDERSTAND THE KING THAT LACKS UNDERSTANDING IS MERELY AN OPPRESSOR.

746

A KING MUST UNDERSTAND THERE CAN BE NO PACTS NOR BINDING OATHS BETWEEN MEN AND LIONS, NOR CAN THE LAMB ENJOY ANY MEETING OF THE MIND WITH THE WOLF.

747

A KING MUST UNDERSTAND EVERY GOOD QUALITY HAS ITS DARK SHADOW, AND NOTHING GOOD CAN COME INTO THIS WORLD WITHOUT AT ONCE PRODUCING ITS CORRESPONDING EVIL.

748

A KING MUST UNDERSTAND THERE IS NOTHING SO ADVANTAGEOUS TO MANKIND AS A GOOD KING, AND NOTHING SO HARMFUL AS AN EVIL ONE.

749

A KING MUST UNDERSTAND EVEN THE MOST DEADLY, DANGEROUS, AND HATEFUL PERSON HAS A SOFT SPOT SOMEWHERE THAT IS VULNERABLE AND CAPABLE OF BEING ABSORBED BY LOVE.

750

A KING MUST UNDERSTAND TO POUR LOVE ON HATE IS LIKE POURING WATER ON A FIRE.

751

A KING MUST UNDERSTAND POWERFUL MEN TEND TO BE INTENSE AND PENSIVE.

752

A KING MUST UNDERSTAND HE WHO IS ARROGANT IS ALSO IGNORANT, OTHERWISE ARROGANCE WOULD NOT BE HIS

753

A KING MUST UNDERSTAND IT TAKES PATIENCE AND DETERMINATION TO ATTAIN CERTAIN LEVELS IN LIFE.

754

A KING MUST UNDERSTAND EVERYTHING THAT RESULTS IN SOMETHING BEAUTIFUL IS BEAUTIFUL IN AND OF ITSELF.

755

A KING MUST UNDERSTAND THERE IS NOTHING THAT CAN HAPPEN TO YOU THAT CAN PREVENT YOU FROM BEING KIND, MAGNANIMOUS, JUST, OR SELF-CONTROLLED.

756

A KING MUST UNDERSTAND SUCCESS IS THE RESULT OF ONE'S EFFORT TO PERSONIFY EXCELLENCE.

757

A KING MUST UNDERSTAND HE WHO HAS A LOT OF UNDERSTANDING IS ALWAYS HUMBLE.

758

A KING MUST UNDERSTAND WHEREVER YOU SEE HUMILITY, KNOW THAT **UNDERSTANDING** IS PRESENT ALSO.

759

A KING MUST UNDERSTAND PEOPLE OFTEN DEPLOY CYNICISM AS AN ATTEMPT TO DISGUISE THEIR FEELINGS OF INSECURITY AND FEAR.

760

A KING MUST UNDERSTAND DOUBT IS A TREACHEROUS FOE THAT SHALL CAUSE YOU TO LOSE THE WAR BY CONVINCING YOU NOT TO FIGHT.

761

A KING MUST UNDERSTAND THE FEAR OF CRITICISM IS A THIEF THAT SHALL STEAL YOUR KINGDOM BY ROBBING YOU OF YOUR INITIATIVE.

762

A KING MUST UNDERSTAND THE FEAR OF CRITICISM IS NAUGHT BUT THE INTERNALIZED FEAR OF THE OPINIONS OF

OTHERS.

763

A KING MUST UNDERSTAND THE SPEECH OF A MAN IS A MANIFESTATION OF THE MIND OF THAT MAN.

764

A KING MUST UNDERSTAND SMALL OPPORTUNITIES ARE OFTEN THE BEGINNING OF GREAT ENTERPRISES.

765

A KING MUST UNDERSTAND THE DESIRE TO BE VICTORIOUS IS NOTHING WITHOUT THE DESIRE TO PREPARE.

766

A KING MUST UNDERSTAND A KING IS THE ARCHITECT OF HIS OWN DESTINY AND THE AUTHOR OF HIS OWN STORY.

767

A KING MUST UNDERSTAND IN WAR, TO NEVER TELL YOUR ENEMY YOUR PLANS, IS TO NEVER GIVE HIM HIS WISH.

768

A KING MUST UNDERSTAND OF TWO CLOSE FRIENDS, WHOEVER KNOWS ONE, IMMEDIATELY ASSUMES THE OTHER TO BE OF THE SAME CHARACTER.

769

A KING MUST UNDERSTAND IT IS WRONG FOR A KING TO BE ALWAYS AT WAR, AND TO NOT SEEK PEACE AS AN OBJECTIVE. FOR WAR IS MEANT TO LEAD TO PEACE, JUST AS TOIL IS MEANT TO LEAD TO REST.

770

A KING MUST UNDERSTAND HE WHO CHERISHES A BEAUTIFUL VISION AND HOLDS A LOFTY IDEAL IN HIS HEART SHALL ONE DAY SEE HIS ASPIRATIONS COME TO PASS.

771

A KING MUST UNDERSTAND YOU MUST TRAIN YOURSELF TO REMAIN CALM IN SPITE OF THE STORMS OF LIFE. FOR BY DOING THIS, YOU SHALL BECOME THE LIGHTHOUSE THAT GUIDES ALL OTHER SHIPS TO SAFETY.

772

A KING MUST UNDERSTAND THERE HAS NEVER BEEN A CIVILIZATION WHOSE DESIGN WAS BASED UPON CHAOS.

773

A KING MUST UNDERSTAND ANGER AND ITS FOLLOWING CONSEQUENCES ARE MUCH MORE HARMFUL THAN THOSE THINGS THAT MADE YOU ANGRY.

774

A KING MUST UNDERSTAND GREED IS A FORCE THAT IS POWERFUL ENOUGH TO BLIND A MAN TO ANYTHING.

775

A KING MUST UNDERSTAND THERE IS NO PREDATOR ALIVE THAT CAN ATTACK WHAT IT CANNOT SEE.

776

A KING MUST UNDERSTAND HE WHO AVOIDS ALL RISKS, TRADES FULFILLMENT FOR THE ILLUSION OF SAFETY.

777

A KING MUST UNDERSTAND THAT WHICH HAS TAKEN YEARS TO DEVELOP SHALL TAKE TIME TO UNDO.

778

A KING MUST UNDERSTAND EVEN THE VERY WISE CANNOT SEE THE ENDS OF ALL BEGINNINGS.

779

A KING MUST UNDERSTAND A MAN HAS ALWAYS IN HIS POWER THE ABILITY TO SEE HIMSELF, SHAPE HIMSELF, AND BECOME WHATEVER HE WILLS.

780

A KING MUST UNDERSTAND POWER IS NEVER FREELY GIVEN. IT MUST ALWAYS BE EARNED.

781

A KING MUST UNDERSTAND POWER IS THE ULTIMATE CURRENCY. FOR WITH IT YOU SHALL BE ABLE TO PURCHASE WHATEVER YOU DESIRE.

782

A KING MUST UNDERSTAND YOU MUST ALWAYS BE THE
MASTER OF YOUR OWN IMAGE RATHER THAN ALLOWING
OTHERS TO SHAPE IT FOR YOU.

783

A KING MUST UNDERSTAND YOU MUST ALWAYS HOLD
YOURSELF IN AWE OR ELSE NONE SHALL.

784

A KING MUST UNDERSTAND WHEN THE SHEPHERD FALLS,
ALL OF THE SHEEP SHALL SCATTER.

785

A KING MUST UNDERSTAND SELF-INTEREST IS THE
MIGHTIEST MOTIVE OF ALL.

786

A KING MUST UNDERSTAND YOU MUST LEARN TO EXPLOIT
THE CHAOS OF THE WORLD RATHER THAN SUCCUMB TO IT.

787

A KING MUST UNDERSTAND POWER LIES NOT ONLY IN WHAT YOU HAVE, BUT ALSO IN WHAT OTHERS BELIEVE THAT YOU MIGHT HAVE.

788

A KING MUST UNDERSTAND PREVENTING YOUR ENEMIES FROM SEEING THE PURPOSE OF YOUR ACTIONS SHALL ALWAYS GIVE YOU THE ADVANTAGE OVER THEM.

789

A KING MUST UNDERSTAND ULTIMATE POWER CONSISTS IN HAVING OTHERS MOVE IN THE DIRECTION THAT YOU DESIRE WITHOUT THEM REALIZING IT.

790

A KING MUST UNDERSTAND YOU MUST NEVER GET INTO AN ARGUMENT OVER SOMETHING THAT IS NONE OF YOUR BUSINESS.

791

A KING MUST UNDERSTAND THE ONLY THING THAT CAN

792

A KING MUST UNDERSTAND YOU MUST NEVER ALLOW HURTFUL WORDS TO ACCOMPANY A GIFT.

793

A KING MUST UNDERSTAND YOU SHALL NEVER CONVINCE ANOTHER TO LOVE YOU BY BEING HATEFUL TOWARDS THEM.

794

A KING MUST UNDERSTAND KNOWLEDGE IS THE GATEKEEPER TO THE REALM OF UNDERSTANDING.

795

A KING MUST UNDERSTAND NO ONE MAKES ENEMIES BY BEING GENEROUS.

796

A KING MUST UNDERSTAND KINGS WERE MADE TO BE HONORABLE. THEREFORE, YOU SHOULD DESIRE NOTHING

797

A KING MUST UNDERSTAND TO BE KIND IS ALWAYS IN YOUR **POWER**.

798

A KING MUST UNDERSTAND HE WHO FROM FEAR HESITATES TO MAKE A DECISION, EVEN THOUGH HE HAS ALL OF THE NECESSARY FACTS AT HAND, SHALL NEVER ACCOMPLISH ANYTHING.

799

A KING MUST UNDERSTAND HE WHO DOUBTS MAKES NO PROGRESS.

800

A KING MUST UNDERSTAND WILLPOWER IS DIRECTLY TIED TO WHAT ONE BELIEVES IS POSSIBLE.

801

A KING MUST UNDERSTAND CREATIVITY FLOURISHES

UNDER PRESSURE IN THOSE WHO HAVE STRONG MINDS.

802

A KING MUST UNDERSTAND YOU, WITH YOUR OWN MIND,
MUST LEARN TO MAKE YOUR OWN PARADISE.

803

A KING MUST UNDERSTAND NO TREE HAS BRANCHES SILLY
ENOUGH TO FIGHT EACH OTHER.

804

A KING MUST UNDERSTAND THE WORST CONFUSION
IMAGINABLE, IS THE CONFUSION BORNE OF PANIC.

805

A KING MUST UNDERSTAND PEACE IS THE END OF
IGNORANCE.

806

A KING MUST UNDERSTAND IF YOU TRULY GAIN AN
UNDERSTANDING OF THE FACT THAT EVERYONE
MANUFACTURES THEIR OWN DISCONTENT, NO ONE CAN

HINDER YOU BUT YOURSELF, AND EVERYTHING DEPENDS
UPON YOUR VIEW OF IT, YOU SHALL HAVE PEACE AND **LOVE**
TILL THE END OF YOUR DAYS.

807

A KING MUST UNDERSTAND IT IS ONLY ONCE A MAN
MAKES A COMMITMENT TO SEEING THAT HIS EYES SHALL
OPEN.

808

A KING MUST UNDERSTAND YOU DO VIOLENCE TO
YOURSELF WHENEVER YOU SCORN ANOTHER OR SEEK TO
HARM ANOTHER OUT OF ANGER.

809

A KING MUST UNDERSTAND IF YOU **LOVE** SIMPLY FOR
THE JOY OF LOVING, THAT JOY SHALL NEVER FALL AWAY.
HOWEVER, IF YOU **LOVE** ONLY FOR THE SAKE OF WAITING
ON SOMETHING IN RETURN, IN TIME, YOU SHALL SURELY BE
DISAPPOINTED.

810

A KING MUST UNDERSTAND IN ORDER TO CREATE GREATNESS IN YOUR KINGDOM, YOU MUST REPLACE ALL OF THE FEAR THAT YOU POSSESS WITH **UNDERSTANDING** AND **FAITH** IN YOURSELF.

811

A KING MUST UNDERSTAND WHEN YOU CEASE TO FEAR WORLDLY **POWER**, A FAR GREATER **POWER** SHALL ARRIVE TO SUPPORT YOU.

812

A KING MUST UNDERSTAND MASTERING THE ABILITY TO BE SERENE IN AN ADVERSE SITUATION IS THE SAME THING AS FINDING THE COURAGE TO FACE IT.

813

A KING MUST UNDERSTAND DESTINY SENDS ONE'S ENEMIES AS A TEST BY WHICH THEY MAY GAUGE THEIR **STRENGTH**.

814

A KING MUST UNDERSTAND YOU MUST NEVER LUST PRIVATELY AFTER THAT WHICH YOU WOULD BE ASHAMED TO SEEK OPENLY.

815

A KING MUST UNDERSTAND THE MORE YOU LOVE, THE MORE LOVABLE YOU SHALL BECOME.

816

A KING MUST UNDERSTAND EVERYTHING THAT IS ALIVE FEARS THAT WHICH IS STRANGE.

817

A KING MUST UNDERSTAND THERE ARE NO ACCIDENTS AND THERE ARE NO COINCIDENCES. FOR ALL LIVE IN ACCORDANCE WITH A GREATER PLAN, AND EVERYTHING HAPPENS FOR A REASON.

818

A KING MUST UNDERSTAND ARROGANCE IS A CLEVER DISGUISE FOR DEEP-SEATED PAIN AND INSECURITY.

819

A KING MUST UNDERSTAND YOU MUST DO NOTHING, NOT EVEN THE SMALLEST THING AS IF YOU CONSIDERED IT UNIMPORTANT.

820

A KING MUST UNDERSTAND IT IS BY FLEEING THE HUNTER THAT THE FRIGHTENED RABBIT IS ENSNARED BY HIS TRAP.

821

A KING MUST UNDERSTAND GREATNESS FEARS NO CONSEQUENCES.

822

A KING MUST UNDERSTAND THE DESIRE FOR SAFETY AND SECURITY STANDS AGAINST EVERY GREAT AND NOBLE ENTERPRISE.

823

A KING MUST UNDERSTAND A WEAKENED MIND SEES EVERYTHING THROUGH A DARKENED VEIL.

824

A KING MUST UNDERSTAND IT IS CRITICAL FOR A KING

TO LEARN TO TAKE CRITICISM WITHOUT TAKING OFFENSE.

825

A KING MUST UNDERSTAND YOU MUST NEVER ALLOW

YOURSELF TO TAKE PART IN GRATUITOUS FAULT-FINDING.

826

A KING MUST UNDERSTAND FEAR AND HESITATION SHALL

PLACE OBSTACLES IN YOUR PATH, WHILE COURAGE SHALL

REMOVE THEM.

827

A KING MUST UNDERSTAND THE WEAPONS THAT ARE

MOST ABLE TO, AND MOST EASILY, CONQUER REASON ARE

TERROR AND VIOLENCE.

828

A KING MUST UNDERSTAND MEN INJURE EITHER FROM

THOUGHTS OF FEAR, OR THOUGHTS OF HATRED.

829

A KING MUST UNDERSTAND INSTEAD OF SEEING THE

DIFFICULTY IN EVERY OPPORTUNITY, YOU MUST TRAIN

YOURSELF TO SEE THE OPPORTUNITY IN EVERY DIFFICULTY.

830

A KING MUST UNDERSTAND IN ORDER TO BE KING,

YOU MUST FIRST LOOK AT THE WORLD THROUGH THE EYES

OF A KING.

IV

ALTHOUGH HE WAS ONCE FORSAKEN IN HIS KINGDOM

BEHOLD, I HAVE REFINED THEE, BUT NOT WITH SILVER; I

HAVE CHOSEN THEE IN THE FURNACE OF AFFLICTION.

(ISAIAH 48:10)

In order for the **KING** in a man to be born, the boy in him must die. For without death, there can be no resurrection. Death is always a painful experience. However, it is necessary, for death is what allows new life to spring forth, and replace old outdated forms with new fresh ones. It is only by **UNDERSTANDING** this truth that one can muster the courage to face death courageously, and see it for the illusion that it is. For nothing truly dies. Death is merely a change of form. It is the dropping of one garment and replacing it with a new one. Much like a snake must periodically shed its skin so that it may grow. To experience death is to feel forsaken. It is to feel abandoned and left alone. For all experience death alone. It is only once one makes it through to the other side of death, which is rebirth, that they shall see and understand that **LOVE** shall never forsake you. The pain of death only makes it appear to do so. It is **LOVE** that guides us through death, for **LOVE** desires us to grow. And thus it was that I, the child, had to die, and be forsaken by my kingdom, so that I, the **KING**

COULD RULE IT. I, THE BOY, HAD TO BE ABANDONED, DISCOUNTED, AND MURDERED BY HEARTBREAK, SO THAT I, THE **KING**, COULD RISE FROM THE ASHES LIKE THE PHOENIX TO STEP INTO THE MAJESTIC EFFULGENCE OF NOBILITY. AND NOW THE BOY THAT WAS LEFT FOR DEAD HAS RETURNED **KING**.

1
FATHER FORSAKEN

FATHER, FATHER, WHAT HAVE I DONE,

TO MAKE YOU FORSAKE YOUR ONE AND ONLY SON.

I'VE SOUGHT OUT YOUR LOVE, AS IF FOR BURIED

TREASURE,

PAID FOR IT WITH MY HEART, KEPT A RECORD IN MY MIND'S

LEDGER.

YET, NO MATTER WHAT PRICE I MAY PAY ALL I RECEIVE IS

REJECTION,

SHAME, RAGE, EMBARRASSMENT, AND MY FAMILIAR FRIEND,

DEJECTION.

I HAVEN'T BEEN FAULTLESS, SO I MUST ACCEPT MY SHARE OF

BLAME,

MY FEAR IS THAT HATE SHALL POLLUTE MY ESSENCE, AND IT

Shall never be the same.

2
CAPTURED

Another day in hell, searching for heaven in the pit,

Desperately seeking all the KNOWLEDGE and

WISDOM I can possibly get.

When a sage's jewel is gained, another key to heaven

is received,

But a deeper passage to perdition is uncovered when

it is not used or perceived.

As the cycle starts again and the day comes anew,

Unending bouts with monotony, endeavors to find

something new.

Repetitious ventures, spliced with fortuitous

occasions,

Life's scabrous road steered by mundane persuasions.

Concentrated conditions bring exaggerated

renditions,

As reality is absolved of insignificant traditions.

Protracted anxiety, unending for some,

Imprudent prayers, for another day to come.

Another day comes, a blessing or curse in disguise,

As I wonder what new atrocity shall I witness with

my eyes.

What new joy shall I find under the sun?

My hope whispers plenty, while despair screams none.

As day turns to night, and night turns to day,

I stick my chest out in defiance, and then wipe the

tears away,

They'll never take me alive, at least that's what they

say,

The living are dead, and the dead are living in the

place that I stay.

Locked behind a door, hidden from existence,

Chained behind a fence, a victim of resistance.

Subjugated amongst the oblivious, an abducted

generation,

Having nightmares of powerful demons soliciting
liberation.

Lost souls wandering aimlessly in a guarded tomb,

Victims of a dependency not felt since the womb.

Tarnished gems, robbed of their brilliance,

Uncut diamonds, revered for resilience.

Senseless battles being fought in an unwinnable war,

Worthy adversaries exposed, revealed to be subpar.

Folly's unmistakable voice being echoed, heard again
and again,

Allies found wanting of virtue, the cause of
chagrin.

Attempts being made to polish memory's mirror,

Reflections being reviewed to see things clearer.

Incessant chatter being employed to divert agony's
river,

Suffering's frigid baptism causing fervent souls to

SHIVER.

Death's issues being pondered to ease apprehension's
embrace,

Righteousness being annihilated, vanishing without
a trace.

On the path to destruction, undiscerning to the
fact,

Desensitized to reality, unwilling to react.

Lost behind an image, on a quest for control,

Witless to the marring being done to the soul.

Lucid indirections, enlivened by demonic intention,

Oxygen taken from the air, replaced by stale tension.

Confused by the desire for the very things that
destroy,

Angels being duped, falling for the devil's ploy.

3

LOST LOVE'S BITTERSWEET MEMORIES

Ghost of love's past, a cruel, despicable specter,

Stagnant minds and broken hearts, allowing misery

to fester.

Haunting tortured souls without the burden of

remorse,

Feeding on the very emotions of which they are the

source.

Dealing with lost LOVE as my weaknesses are

exposed to be,

If I knew it would have hurt this much, I would

never have let her close to me.

Frivolous consequences adding depth to my despair,

Surviving on tribulation, lungs breathing without

air.

Manifestations of misery, forbidden from my eyes,

Melancholy immortalized as this ballad cries.

How could the most bitter taste I've ever known
come from the sweetest sugar I've ever tasted?

Silently attempting not to mourn, grieving for
dreams that have been wasted.

Washing my soul with anguish as karma is
manifested,

Expelling pride slowly as my delicate heart is tested.

Growth is rooted in change, although change does
not promise growth,

How unfortunate it is that sorrow seems always to
accompany both.

Spirit being frozen during the coldest winter ever,

Patience being gained as I await better weather.

Scars of my past giving way to the pain of today,

Lost in broken heartedness as I search for my way.

4

REALITY

As the line becomes obscured between friend and foe,

Reality becomes blurred as one struggles to grow.

Imaginary loves lost to circumstances unknown,

Prodigious prices being paid for ascension to the

throne.

Spiritual POWER being gained as adversity is

overcome,

DIVINE warfare taking place, unbeknownst to

some.

Horrible storms being weathered as KNOWLEDGE

is gained,

Heart becoming hardened as calamities are rained.

Differences between ignorance and WISDOM

slowly being learned,

As old presumptions and fraudulent maxims are

expeditiously burned.

Promiscuous promises being made to destinies unfulfilled,

Souls crying out in anguish as dreams are being killed.

Unceasing desires restrained by finite possibilities,

While boundless ambitions are willed with limited capabilities.

5

PAIN

I'm crying inside, I pray the tears don't seep out,

I'm beginning to understand what pain is all about.

Pain is when your joy is purposely snatched away,

Pain is when happiness flees your presence every single day.

Pain is when you're not sick, yet searching for a cure,

Pain is constantly being told to try and endure.

Pain is when those around you are seemingly unaware,

Pain is constantly wondering does anyone care.

6
HOPE

They say home is where the heart is, but I don't think that this is so,

I say home is where hope is, because that's where I want to go.

Hope is where freedom resides and LOVE always makes room,

Hope is where jealousy dies and hate's fires cannot fume.

Hope follows loyalty and is led by conviction,

Hope never gives up or permits dereliction.

Hope allows you to thrive and makes it easy to cope,

That's why home can't be where my heart is, because where my heart is there's no hope.

7
PATIENCE, PLEASE

Patience, please come save me. Help me find my way,

Patience, please give me your STRENGTH. I have to face another day.

Patience, please give me the determination to

OVERCOME MY PLIGHT,

PATIENCE, PLEASE GIVE ME THE WISDOM TO KNOW

WHEN NOT TO FIGHT.

PATIENCE, PLEASE GIVE ME THE POWER TO WIN EVERY

BATTLE,

PATIENCE, PLEASE GIVE ME POISE SO I MAY BE IMPOSSIBLE TO

RATTLE.

PATIENCE, YOU'RE A VIRTUE. I'VE LEARNED THAT THIS IS SO,

BUT IT WOULD BE SO MUCH EASIER TO EMBRACE YOU IF

YOUR COMPANION WASN'T SLOW.

8

SNOWFLAKES IN HELL

I ONCE WENT TO THE LORD AND I ASKED HIM,

"GOD, JUST HOW CAN A SNOWFLAKE STAY FROZEN IN HELL,

AND STAY TRUE TO THE HEAVENS FROM WHICH IT FELL?"

HE SAID, "SON, SUCCESS IS GAINED BY GAINING

KNOWLEDGE WHICH IS POWER,

WHILE FAILURE IS PROMISED WITH THE PASSING OF EACH

IDLE HOUR.

SELF-DESTRUCTION IS BOUGHT WITH THE PURCHASE OF

FOOLISH PRIDE,

While WISDOM is humbly obtained by learning to

take pain in stride.

Fear not your troubles, for they give you the

opportunity to acquire,

The KNOWLEDGE of how to remain cool in the

devil's blistering fire."

9

BUTTERFLIES

Caged in a cocoon, anxious to be free,

Wondering what I shall grow to be.

Eager to show my colors, brightened by adversity's

dye,

Anxious to flap my wings and begin to fly.

Evolving in this cocoon, anxious to see,

The beautiful creature I shall emerge to be.

10

KING PERSEVERANCE

KING Perseverance the powerful,

The cornerstone of all success,

The ally that all men must unite with,

If they desire to be their best.

In order to rule, a KING must keep you in his

possession,

For you are the most essential guide in one's quest

for perfection.

Without you, men falter and fall short of their

goal,

In your absence, the strong stumble and lose all

control.

You're always there pleading for the restless to stay

the course,

While failure constantly threatens them with

bittersweet remorse.

Victory is always accompanied by persistence and

tenacity,

While ambition guides her course with its insistent

voracity.

11
BLOOMING OF A FLOWER

A flower is blossoming, does anyone care?

Its petals are blooming, is anyone aware?

Denied the sun, it struggles to survive,

Ignored and mistreated, yet it manages to thrive.

It endures brutal coldness and excruciating heat,

Still it musters the audacity to bloom in concrete.

EPILOGUE

Who am I? What is my purpose? These are the questions that all who are seeking to attain true greatness must eventually ask and have answered if they are ever to reach their highest potential. For it is these questions that lead one to not only discover their place in the world, but also to discover Truth, which is the foundation of all achievement. While some float through life never asking these questions at all or perhaps asking them but never seriously seeking an answer, those who sincerely ask these questions and seek wholeheartedly to unravel the mysteries of their existence undoubtedly find that for which they seek. For the answers to these questions themselves lie hidden in the genuine search for them.

It was over ten years ago, in 2009, that I was forced to search out an answer to these questions, as I was confronted with a situation in which my life depended upon me doing so. After going to trial and unjustly being convicted of the crimes of 1st degree burglary and assault and battery with intent to kill, I was sentenced to fifteen years in a maximum-security prison. Fortunately, I had to do only nine years of this sentence as I was released early due to a miscarriage of justice inflicted upon me during my trial.

During my first few months in prison at McCormick Correctional Institution, as I was still trying to make sense of my plight, I found myself in the middle of a debate between two individuals who I politicked with on a daily basis whose names were Slim and K.O. There was nothing particularly strange about this, as frivolous debates are very common in prison and due to my quiet nature, I was often the appointed adjudicator in a great many of these debates. On this particular day, I sided with Slim's position in the debate. This angered K.O. to the point where he venomously said, "Who is Troy? Who the fuck is Troy?" It was then that I was faced with a decision that marked a major turning point in my life. In prison, what K.O. said and particularly the way that

HE SAID IT WAS TREMENDOUSLY DISRESPECTFUL. THUS, I WAS PRESENTED WITH THE CHOICE TO EITHER ADDRESS THIS PERCEIVED INSULT IN THE TYPICAL PRISON FASHION, WHICH WOULD HAVE ENDED IN BLOODSHED OR THE POTENTIAL LOSS OF LIFE, OR I COULD EXPLORE MY FEELINGS AND ATTEMPT TO DISCOVER WHY IT WAS THAT I HAD FELT SO OFFENDED. WISELY CHOOSING TO EXAMINE MY FEELINGS, I IMMEDIATELY SAW THAT THE REASON THAT I FELT THE WAY THAT I FELT ABOUT WHAT WAS SAID WAS BECAUSE I DIDN'T KNOW WHO TROY WAS. I ONLY KNEW WHO OTHERS HAD SAID THAT I WAS SUPPOSED TO BE. IT WAS THEN FOR THE VERY FIRST TIME IN MY LIFE THAT I DEFINED MYSELF. THIS WAS THE ORIGIN OF THE DIVINE KING MANTRA.

THEREFORE, BY DEFINING MYSELF, I HAD CROWNED MYSELF KING. IT WAS THEN THAT I SET MYSELF UPON THE JOURNEY TO DISCOVER JUST EXACTLY WHAT IT MEANT TO BE KING. BY MAKING THIS DECISION TO SEARCH OUT THE TRUE MEANING OF WHAT A KING WAS, DUE TO THE LAW OF ATTRACTION, A MEANS TO MAKE THIS DISCOVERY WAS SOON MADE AVAILABLE TO ME. ONE OF THE FIRST CLUES WHICH THE UNIVERSE PRESENTED ME WITH CAME IN THE FORM OF A QUOTE THAT I RANDOMLY HEARD FROM ONE OF MY FELLOW

INMATES.

WHILST SEEMINGLY ALL WHO SURROUNDED ME CONTINUED TO EXIST IN THE REALITY OF PRISON, I BEGAN TO INTERACT WITH MY ENVIRONMENT AS IF IT WAS A UNIVERSITY. THE SUBJECT THAT I CHOSE TO MAJOR IN WAS THE ART OF KINGSHIP. FROM THAT DAY FORTH, FOR NINE STRAIGHT YEARS, I DEDICATED MYSELF TO 12 TO 14-HOUR DAYS OF INCESSANT STUDY UPON THE SUBJECT, READING EVERYTHING FROM THE WORKS OF ROBERT GREENE TO THE WRITINGS OF NICCOLÒ MACHIAVELLI. STUDYING EVERYTHING FROM THE HERMETIC TEACHINGS OF THE KYBALION TO THE WISDOM OF THE BHAGAVAD GITA. RESEARCHING THOROUGHLY EVERYTHING RANGING FROM THE INSTRUCTIONS OF LAO-TZU TO THE MEDITATIONS OF MARCUS AURELIUS.

WHILE INDEED AT TIMES MY VORACIOUS APPETITE FOR UNDERSTANDING DREW UPON ME THE SCORN AND RIDICULE OF THOSE SURROUNDING ME WHO COULD NOT FATHOM WHY I WOULD BE WASTING VALUABLE TIME ATTEMPTING TO BETTER MYSELF, THE FIRE OF MY PURPOSE LEFT ME IMPERVIOUS TO THEIR TAUNTS. THE MORE KNOWLEDGE I ATTAINED, THE MORE I BEGAN TO BE SOUGHT OUT AND

REVERED FOR IT. EVENTUALLY I WENT FROM PLAYING THE ROLE OF STUDENT TO THAT OF TEACHER AND, MUCH LIKE JOSEPH FROM THE BIBLE, FOUND MYSELF ENTRUSTED TO SEVERAL POSITIONS OF LEADERSHIP INSIDE OF THE PRISON.

AS I CONTINUED TO STUDY MORE AND MORE, MOLDING MY MIND INTO THAT OF A TRUE KING, ONE OF THE THINGS THAT I QUICKLY DISCOVERED WAS THAT IT IS A KING'S RESPONSIBILITY TO INSPIRE THEIR PEOPLE AND SHARE ALL KNOWLEDGE GAINED WITH THEM SO THAT THEY MAY USE THIS KNOWLEDGE AS A PLATFORM FOR THEIR OWN GREATNESS.

ABOUT THE AUTHOR

Antionelle Owens, an inspirational speaker, entrepreneur, and spiritual advisor, was born in Orangeburg, South Carolina, but raised in the early part of his life in St. Matthews before moving to Columbia in his adolescence. He attended A.C. Flora High School, where he played basketball for the late Don Bell. Antionelle earned a scholarship and majored in Political Science at King University in Bristol, Tennessee.

After college, he spent a year coaching girls' basketball at Crayton Middle School in Columbia, SC. He then had the opportunity to play basketball professionally in Lausanne, Switzerland. After returning home from this experience, different circumstances began to push him towards discovering his true purpose by arranging it so that he would have to spend time with the downtrodden in prison.

This is what led Antionelle to author the kingship initiation series which he has entitled, *Chronicles of the KING*, of which the three books, *Prince Micah the Magnificent, A KING MUST UNDERSTAND: Thoughts of a Divine King: A Manual Concerning the Art of Kingship*, and *For He Comes Out of Prison to be King* are a part.